P9-ECN-787

wandering time

Camino del Sol

A Chicana and Chicano Literary Series

wandering time:
western notebooks

LUIS ALBERTO URREA

The University of Arizona Press   Tucson

The University of Arizona Press
© 1999 Luis Alberto Urrea
First Printing

♾ This book is printed on acid-free, archival-quality paper.
Manufactured in the United States of America

04   03   02   01   00   99   6   5   4   3   2   1

Library of Congress Cataloging-in-Publication Data

Urrea, Luis Alberto.
Wandering time: Western notebooks/Luis Alberto Urrea.
p. cm.– (Camino del sol)
ISBN 0-8165-1866-1 (acid-free, archival-quality paper)
1. Urrea, Luis Alberto–Journeys–West (U.S.)   2. Authors,
American–20th century–Biography.   3. West (U.S.)–
Description and travel.   I. Title.   II. Series.
PS3571.R74 Z476 1999   98-25439
818'.5403–ddc21   CIP
[B]

British Library Cataloguing-in-Publication Data
A catalogue record for this book is available from the British
Library.

"Hill Farm," from *Sumerian Vistas* by A. R. Ammons. ©1987
A. R. Ammons. Reprinted by permission of W. W. Norton &
Company, Inc.
"Envoy" by Wendell Berry. Reprinted with permission.

For Cinderella—
fairytales can come true.

Glorious it is
When wandering time is come.

—Alaskan Eskimo song

contents

acknowledgments

Thanks, first and foremost, to my bride Cinderella. Her aspen-grove eyes lit a dark era and brought me to these words. This book is hers.

And to my friend and invaluable critical reader, Brian Andrew Laird.

To the next round of readers: Kathy Allen, Darrell Bourque, Tony Delcavo, Jonna Faulkner, Pam Moser, Karen Reese, Steve Rossman.

To the critical readers who first reviewed the manuscript: Patricia Preciado Martin and Richard Shelton.

And to the editor who first brought it to life: Martha Moutray. Thanks also to Team UA, especially Judith, Chris, Kathryn, Lisa, and Christopher.

Stewart O'Nan: you remind me daily to love this world.

The writing communities of wild America keep the mountains alive in me. Thanks to my homeys in: Colorado, New Mexico, West Texas, the West Coast from Tijuana to Anchorage, Southern Arizona, Mexico City, and Cajun Louisiana.

And a special thanks to Dr. Doris Meriwether and the University of Southwest Louisiana.

May my teachers and elders and ancestors smile upon this work.

Viva Teresita Urrea, la Santa de Cabora.

wandering time

introductory matters:

bones in
good motion

You would have to care about the ground. And you would have to care about the words. This is what I'm getting at: mud and verbs. Breathe one into the other and you stumble into a tiny Genesis. It's our little secret. It's a secret worth sharing.

Allow me to offer you an example.

In *Black Sun,* the one book in which he truly allowed himself to be tender, Edward Abbey wrote a beautiful paragraph about my favorite tree, the aspen. Aspens, aside from instilling in me an inexplicable melancholic joy along with a nostalgia for lives that were not my own, also remind me of the word *love.* Anyone who has ever engaged an aspen in any meaningful dialogue at all recognizes its optimistic and generous nature almost immediately.

Take Ed, for example:

> He heard voices but did not halt his work. He often heard voices in this part of the forest. The fine leaves of the aspens, delicately suspended, shimmered like water under light, shivered and tinkled like glass bells with the slightest breeze, and their rustling all together resembled the whispering of voices, murmurs, speech without words.

Forget Ed Abbey's imperfections and indelicacies. How could I not love a writer who wrote that paragraph? How could I not want to step up to the plate and take a swing at writing something as pure and sweet and true? And how could I not want to live in a place where slender white and goldgreen trees turn silver in light, quiver like the surface of a mercury stream, and seem to sigh poems in the breeze? I can't live long without either of their good company—the words or the trees.

Other things I can't seem to do without for very long: cottonwoods, lodgepole pines, columbines, buffalo (*tatanka*), elk (*wapiti*), snow, lightning, waterfalls, the occasional golden eagle, abandoned homesteads, Jeep trails, trout streams—though I have never fished in my life and wouldn't care to start now. Oh, yes—and bighorns, glaciers, small reflecting lakes giddy with lily pads, hoodoos, monuments, diners, highways, tight mountain roads, and horses—though the last time I rode a horse, it was a tired Sioux mare being led around a pasture by my patient and somehow un-giggling Oglala brother, Duane. The whole event made me feel like a kindergartener at a pony ride.

Did I mention deer, those gangly forest rats? Did I mention various blood-thirsty and uninterested creatures, like bears and coyotes and lions and rumored wild wolves? Don't forget bats. Bats and skunks and porcupines. There is also something to be said for good, honest buffalo meat at the supermarket. And the occasional addled mountain hippie. And Tom Horn's grave. And Devil's Tower. And the Rockies, once known as The Great Stony Mountains, where nervous white folks descend like snowdrifts to escape people with surnames like mine.

It's a swell place.

I can't wait to get back.

Aw, hell—it's easy to be miserable, hard to live in joy.

In my soul-dictionary, if aspen translates as *love,* then the intermountain West reads like this: *joy.* That isn't to say I was happy there. A creaky marriage came apart at the seams, for example, and the aspens had nothing much to say about it. Etc.

Still, the land did its best. The creeks on their tumbledown way from peaks to prairies flickered gold dust; though mostly fool's gold, it was right for me because I was being a fool at the time. The beavers caught streams mid-stride and held them for me to take a good long look. Trout in these vivid puddles peered up at me and said, "Get the hell out of here." Lions left me presents all over the slopes—a deer's fetlock here, an elk's jawbone there. The land even gave me snacks on its vast canapé platter—wild apples, crispy streamside herbs, berries, plums.

And the music was swinging: thunder cracks and whip-sawing branches, wapiti cries and the helpless laughter of those thousand creeks, the hymns of the leaves and the rain—that mountain rain, Richard Brautigan once wrote, which falls

> with love
> in its pockets.

I usually walked alone, yet I never lacked for excellent companionship and interesting conversation. Aside from the cheery banter of aspens, there were droll marmots to talk to. Generally affable snakes. Uncertain raccoons. Vain ravens and magnificent preening magpies. Compulsively curious mule deer. Grumpy turtles. Reclusive black widows. And delightfully greedy camp-robber birds, more eager even than blue jays to be your best friend as long as you have a baloney sand-wich in your hand.

As if all that weren't enough, I had the portable miracle of a pen and some blank pages and a scoopful of good words to scatter over them.

And two willing feet.

When you can't walk, drive.
Then walk.

What is that feeling when you're driving away from people and they recede on the plain till you see their specks disappearing?—it's the too-huge world vault-ing over us, and it's good-by. But we lean forward to the next crazy venture beneath the skies.

—*Jack Kerouac*

I had a cat for a while. Her name was Rest Stop. I named her after the roadside toilet where I found her, in Utah high coun-try, dirty white, sleeping like a scribble of old snow beneath a little pine tree. She had a deer tick on her head, and a hole in her side that offered a view into her musculature like a tiny window. Her first meal in who knows how long was a splin-ter of buffalo jerky; I took my old folding knife and cut the bottom out of a plastic Sea World cup and put water in it and she drank the whole thing in quivering gulps.

Then she climbed aboard my Jeep and made a home for herself atop the cooler. We traveled the west like this. She was undisturbed by rock and roll on the stereo. She remained unimpressed by Las Vegas. Occasionally, though, she unleashed an outraged Neil Young yowl when she realized she was speeding along among countless belching trucks, somehow suspended three feet above the rushing ground. She surfed the freeways with aplomb and supervised my writing for several years until some Tucsonan stole her off my front porch. Perhaps she joined a roving band of javelinas and is leading them now to greater triumphs.

The advent of Rest Stop occurred at the tail-end of a 5,000 mile trip. I love travel. I love reading about travel, just as I love reading about Nature and writing. I like to keep moving.

Running streams can't get stagnant.

I hope.

Charles Bukowski once wrote to a younger writer, "Keep your bones in good motion, kid, and quietly consume and digest what is necessary. I think it is not so much important to build a literary thing as it is not to hurt things. I think it is important to be quiet and in love with park benches; solve whole areas of pain by walking across a rug." What good advice. Zen master Buk.

The great haiku poets, Basho most famous among them, took impossible walking tours. On these journeys, they kept walking journals. So did Thoreau. Lewis and Clarke can be said to have kept a whopping walking (canoeing) journal. John Steinbeck and William Least Heat-Moon and Ian Frazier, in their wonderful travel books, essentially followed Basho's ancient example. They were keeping walking journals in trucks. And our bold sisters—Mary Oliver, Annie Dillard, Diane Ackerman, Terry Tempest Williams, Linda Hogan, Linda Hasselstrom, Barbara Kingsolver, to name a few I'd give chocolates to on Valentine's Day—why, they're wandering all over the place. You can't keep them sitting at their desks.

And how about that Ti-Jean Kerouac?

Ed Abbey—well, he kept walking, sitting, snoring, drifting, paddling, lying, boasting, farting, boozing, belching, scratching, pondering, revolutionizing and bitching journals.

Me too. If you're a writer, of course, it's all writing. The whole world is your filing cabinet.

A lot of my own writing comes from the waitress at Ben Frank's restaurant on Sunset in Hollywood. I went in for a midnight supper. Gregg Allman was asleep in one of the booths. I sat at the counter. When she put down my silverware, it was covered in frost. "Ma'am?" I said. "Is this fork frozen?"

"Yeah," she said. "I put it in the freezer."

"Why?"

She leaned over the counter and breathed, "I just wanted to watch it stick to your lips."

I daresay that gal walked at least ten miles with me in the Rockies. She kept reminding me to smile.

Another bit of good advice that I think all writers should take is Buckminster Fuller's koan: "Dare to be naive." That Rocky Mountain wife I lost up there around Grant Place and 9th Street in Boulder used to say that the story of my life should be called *Gullible's Travels*. Maybe, maybe not, though I will admit I have believed everything Nature has told me so far.

Naive Bones in Good Motion.

I first heard Nature whisper in the 'hood.

Enough has been said elsewhere about my transit through the strange stations of the cross: from border to barrio to ghetto to suburb. From Tijuana to the Ivy League. All that.

But even in Tijuana, Nature spoke. She came to us in the fruit trees and the cactus, the robotic ants and the wild birds. Grandmothers and aunties presided over complex and portable farms and gardens planted in brightly painted flower pots. And the pillbugs in the Tijuana hills are as long as your thumb.

Even in the concrete shadow of the projects in Shelltown, Nature stated her case. It was slightly diminished, a bit hushed. But she was there nonetheless, in the form of hummingbirds whirring before the fuchsias, expressing herself in the high and ragged *V*'s of gulls flying out to sea in the afternoons—lit bright orange by sunset, hieroglyphs of impossible freedom.

Imagine my surprise when, one summer, after we had passed through appallingly stinky farmlands and cow pastures, my dad driving through county after county, each radio station greeting us with "Tie Me Kangaroo Down, Sport," we suddenly entered the alien land called Yellowstone. True West! Though, being from San Diego, most of the west was considered "back east."

Not only pine trees, but bears stopping the car. A moose. Geysers. Peaks with this strange stuff all over them—the rangers called it snow.

It was as if God had pulled a pine needle off a tree and put a tattoo on my heart. He used resin for ink. The tattoo says: MOM.

Later, I was lucky enough to go up high and live for a while.

I had a territory, like all good mountain men. For the most part, I stuck to the Front Range looming behind Boulder, Colorado. I chose the Flatirons, Boulder Creek Canyon, Eldorado Springs, Devil's Thumb, some unnamed paths cutting through baffled-cow country, and the Homestead Trail to keep me company. Beyond these were the holy corridors of Rocky Mountain National Park, some forays on Long's Peak, and the amazing windings of Devil's Gulch. Garden of the Gods. Various passes, basins, beaver complexes, groves, ghost towns, abandoned ranches, forts, trails, wallows, gardens, valleys, streams and pronghorn meadows. These started to feel like my own back alley. Certain peaks and trails seemed to call out "Hey, Pal!" when they saw me. Sometimes, they'd invite me in for a cup of coffee.

This small neighborhood has extended north through Wyoming into Montana, northeast into South Dakota, west into Utah, south into New Mexico. Even Arizona—with me not ever imagining it would someday become a temporary home.

All those hilly places. Driving, driving, driving: speeding out the ghastly details of divorce among flitting snowflakes of the Continental Divide. Sweating out the demons of the border on the sunny rocks above Chasm Lake. Grimly flying off on book tour to El Paso and San Antonio until I could hurry back to the peaks.

I considered it my duty to see what was going on. I wasn't after Art, really. I was generally praying. Every page of my notebook tried to say, *Thank you.*

But mostly I was poking around. Climbing higher to get a better look. Reading the plants and the rocks. And reading books. Nothing noble. I was having fun.

It seems to me that a good writer must excel at two things: poking around and paying attention.

Kathleen Dean Moore, in her book *Riverwalking,* says something interesting about this process:

> I wish to speak a word for the art of poking around. Although the art can be practiced in libraries and antique stores and peoples' psyches, the kind of poking around I am interested in advocating must be done outdoors. It is a matter of going into the land to pay close attention, to pry at things with the toe of a boot, to turn over rocks at the edge of a stream and lift boards to look for snakes or the nests of silky deer mice, to kneel close to search out the tiny bones mixed with fur in an animal's scat, to poke a cattail down a gopher hole.
>
> People who poke around have seeds in their socks and rocks in their pockets. They measure things with the span of their hands. They look into the sun when they see a shadow pass across a field. They spit in rivers to make the fish rise. When no one is looking, they may even rub their lips where beavers have

chewed, just to get a sense of it. Often they stand still for a long time, listening, and then they follow the sound, sneaky as a heron, until they are close enough to see a chickadee knocking on wood like a tiny woodpecker. But if the route to the chickadee is crossed by the tracks of a black-tailed deer, they will turn to follow the deer into the firs, unless the deer tracks cross a creek, in which case it is important to meander with the water through the fold between the hills.

Yes indeed, poking around.

As for paying attention, just read any Mary Oliver book you can find. And I like to keep in mind this fragment, from Erica Funkhouser, which thrills me almost as much as the aspens:

> To pay attention
> as lovers pay their debts,
> not in currency
> but in kindness.

The western mountains were very kind to me. They helped me pull my body into a more comfortable fit. Although I will never be anything like a jock, it feels pretty good after a few miles; before that, my own meat chafes me like ill-fitting overalls. (Donald Hall reminds us, "The body is poetry's door.") As I hope to demonstrate here, walking *is* writing.

The landscape peeled back my eyelids and gave me something worth looking at. Once my eyes opened, something deeper and which has no name opened as well. The mountains filled my lungs and mouth with air that tasted sweet. Besides, anything that holds you higher into the sky so the angels can see what you're writing has a lot going for it.

Boy, did I write.

I think notebooks and journals are among our writers' best works. I am more drawn to Cheever's journals, for example, than to his fine stories. Even though the journals are raw and occasionally crude. *Because* they are so. There's still a little bark on them.

Our notebooks, daybooks, workbooks: unadorned and honest . . . more or less. Less composed, at least, and almost spontaneous. I think writing students can learn 100 times more about writing from a writer's diary than from a writer's Pulitzer Prize novel. For me, the notebooks are where the words seem to dance with the most joy. I find myself smiling as I scribble. And I glue all kinds of detritus to the pages. I don't care if it's a jackalope post-card or a butterfly wing. If it delights me, in it goes.

Which, come to think of it, sounds like a fine rule for keeping a notebook.

Han-shan, of Cold Mountain, once wrote:

> The place where I spend my days
> is farther away than I can tell.

I believe him. Every writer lives out beyond the back fence. Out where rivers might run underground, or extinct creatures might yet live, or where the rain never ceases to fall on a neon city. They often struggle for years to get there; there are no road signs or maps or tour guides to show them the way. Some of them are born behind the fence and spend their childhoods poking around in the fragrant weeds and among the rusty wreckage.

It's a strange landscape. It's not always pleasant, but some are fortunate, as I have been at times, to live in Beauty. However they get out there, though, they must always go alone. You have to go alone; there's no other way to learn how to do the work. But Han-shan, and all other writers who get there, spend the rest of their lives sending letters over the fence. Some are paper airplanes, and some are wrapped around stones. They are filled with descriptions of the land and messages from the natives and invitations to come. Come, climb over the fence.

It's the irony of the notebook: we write notes to ourselves, as if we were spending our whole lives trying to tell someone where this place is, this place where we spend our days. Are we telling ourselves? Or are we hoping you will somehow read over our shoulders?

On another day, when he was looking down from Cold Mountain, Han-shan wrote:

> The valleys are long and strewn with stones,
> the streams broad and banked with thick grass.
> Moss is slippery, though no rain has fallen;
> pines sigh, but it isn't the wind.
> Who can break from the snares of the world
> and sit with me among the white clouds?

Before I left Colorado for Arizona, gone south to research a book and retool my soul, I went up to the wide Moraine Valley of Rocky Mountain National Park. If you drive west, along one of the pleasant roads that meander alongside beaver-engineered streams, sooner or later you'll get to groves of trees at the end of the valley. There, if you park and get out and walk south, you'll find lovely bosques of pines and small brush, great knobs of pale stone forming reefs that look like headlands facing a small sea of high-country grasses.

As I walked along, bidding farewell to the land, land I knew I would miss as fiercely and erotically as a lover, I came over a duplex-sized boulder and beheld an elk herd grazing. I sat above them and watched them gliding through the tides of grass like tawny boats. And I crept off the rock and stood on the ground before them. They were mostly cows, and they shied away—but not too shy, nor too far. I stepped forward slowly. They munched and shifted. I began to walk at a regular clip. They swept out around me and settled.

Suddenly, a bull stepped over near me and gave me a good long look at his rack. Antlers as wide as my arms could have reached. He stared at me, planted his feet, and bent down to eat. His big wet eye rolling up at me and his brow serious, but not furious. He was just letting me know he was there. He was the sultan. As long as I didn't get a wild notion to try mating with one of his wives, we'd all be okay.

I sat on a rock and got out my lunch. Me and the elk, enjoying an afternoon snack while snow blew off the far peaks like smoke. Writing a song together.

For just a moment, all pain, all worry and doubt, all clanging of bills and diets and relationships and work and nightmares and politics and career seemed to drift away. It all seemed to be suspended high above us, in a wobbly golden bubble of light. Nothing could touch us. Aspen leaves sighing. No agony at all dared show itself in the valley.

So, fully aware that misery loves miserable company, and joy enjoys solitary freedom, I offer these humble notes. May they hike through your alone time, bring you a small helping of pleasure, a few moments of happiness wherever your mountains may be. Even if you're just walking around the park. Even if your wild country drive is merely the Express Bus or the subway. Even if you're just soaking in the tub after a long day at work. If you listen, you'll hear the aspens—they may be drunk; then again, they may be praying.

Wallace Stevens said:

In my room, the world is beyond my understanding;
But when I walk I see that it consists of three or
four hills and a cloud.

Let's walk to where those little trees are singing.
It is always a song of praise.

spring

Cherry blossoms, more
and more now! Birds have two legs!
Oh, horses have four!
—*Onitsura*

The word for "spring" in Spanish is, of course, *primavera.* A noun that contains the actual object in itself, a noun full of verbs and adjectives. You can hear the rain and the leaves blowing in it, hear the water and the dogs barking in the distance. When I hear *primavera,* not only do I think, *Thank God I'm a writer,* but also, *Thank God I speak Spanish.* "Spring" is simply not enough of a word. "Daisy" is a pale word, while *margarita* has the pungence of the blossom within it. "Butterfly" cannot hope to catch the flutter of brilliant wings like the tiny haiku of *mariposa.* And what's the point, after all, if spring is not full of haiku and brilliant wings?

I finally washed up against the flanks of the Rockies. I hope to stay. Kind of right along the line where the High Plains curl up against the Front Range, like a still wheatgrass beach surge, frozen waves, bemused Arapaho ghosts and medicine spirits looking down upon the BMWs and Jeep "Cherokees" hustling around pointlessly with their car faxes bleeping.

I'm trying to work my roots into this soil, make peace with the ruling spirit of this place, and see what happens.

Easter. Colorado

The top parts of the mountain trail are finally melting out, all slush and snow suddenly gone. I suppose it's a metaphor for resurrection—the friendly path rising from the snow and basking in the sun. Back to life.

Still, feathers of snow. Unbelievably pretty clouds. Aerial icebergs with bruised bellies. The crosses atop the churches rise stark and abandoned against the sky. The ineffable melancholy of the first flakes sneaking in among the spring raindrops. Flakes not even falling. Circling. Seem to be loitering in the air.

———————

I was going up the Resurrected Trail, and the angels were out.

The poison ivy even looked like it was pushing out little flowers. I was moving at a good clip, had gone up about two miles, fresh sweat feeling good lubricating all the cogs, most dark thoughts pushed out by the spice of new spring air.

Ahead, tooling up the trail in electric wheelchairs, a man and a woman. They were accompanied by one of those Canine Companion German shepherds wearing a backpack. Both of them were attractive and laughing. She was blond.

I motored past them and kept on hauling over the bridges that cross the awakening creek. Then up to Fourmile Canyon. Sweat and think and stare at the old ghost truck you can see tucked into the aspens. Then I drifted back down slowly, enjoying the creek. When I got back to the middle bridge, I climbed down near the water and let the riotous sparkles and glimmers transport me.

When I climbed back up, the couple in wheelchairs was waiting, stuck trying to get onto the bridge. The trail had eroded about three inches from the metal lip of the bridge, and they couldn't get their chairs over.

"Can you help us?" she said.

"Sure," I said. "What do I do?"

"Get my front wheels up."

I pulled her up, got her wheels on the lip. Then she instructed me to grab the front of her chair, up near her thighs, and pull. I got hold of her armrest uprights, bent down as I pulled, she worked her little joystick, the motor whined, and she looked into my face about one inch from hers and said, "Oh." I could smell her perfume and her clean clothes. Then she was over the hump.

I went back for him, and he said, "I think you'd better go behind me."

We were he-men: no face-to-face grunting for us.

"Right!" I bellowed.

I grabbed the handles.

"Pop a wheelie," he said. "Just pop me a wheelie."

I popped him an excellent wheelie, fearing for a second that I was going to flip him over. But, feet in the air, he engaged his motor and climbed onto the bridge.

After they'd said their thanks, she asked, "Are you the friendly troll that lives under the bridge? Are you the friendly troll that helps people?"

"That's me," I said.

On down the trail. The Wheelchair Angels had lifted my spirits. I gazed at the amazing peaks and chatted with God. Up ahead, a pleasant-looking fellow sat on a boulder, smiling. Oh no, I thought, reverting immediately to Unfriendly Troll mode, a talkative son of a bitch. I could tell that much from a quarter mile away.

As I reached him, I tried looking away. "Hi!" he said. Shit, I thought.

He wanted to know how far the trail went up. I stopped. I explained distances to him. He revealed that he was from Minnesota. I found myself narrating an edited version of my life story. He was a high school teacher come to Colorado on spring break with his boys. He wore a woven Guatemalan friendship bracelet on his right wrist. Glasses. Richard Dreyfuss beard and hair.

"What do you do?" he asked.

Writer.

Hey—he was a writer too!

Awright, buddeh!

What did I write, he wanted to know. Fiction, non-fiction, what?

A little bit of everything.

Published?

You bet! And you?

Not yet.

One thing led to another and he told me the plot of his hippies-trapped-in-Mexico novel, and I told him he should get an agent, and he said he'd tried but hadn't had any luck, and I told him he should try mine, and he said he didn't have anything to write down the address with, and we ended up squatting beside the trail, scratching the address into the mud with a stick.

I marched away, happier than anything. The Writer and the Wheelchair Angels behind me, no doubt ascending back to Heaven, their work for the day complete.

Me: the Friendly Troll.

We can dream together. . . .
    —*Fields of the Nephilim*

I listen to gothic hellish music in the astonishing morning light of Boulder. I am overwhelmed by being here, by my own history. I came hoping to study and to perfect my work . . . to learn from some masters here.

On the surface, I smile. I'm Mr. Blonde Mejicano: I have a certain sheen, I care, I'm sensitive and spry. Inside me, though, there is another landscape. If you were to look into my heart, you would find a sparkling obsidian chip. And if you were to look into that chip, you would see reflected a desert plain. A wide, desert hardpan, where the wind howls and rags are always fluttering. I live in that desert.

I walk in a world of ghosts. All the *curanderismo* and Indian strangeness of my boyhood dogs me; Teresita Urrea, La Santa de Cabora, whispers to me; I am haunted by the witch's breasts I touched in third grade; God in His many-colored coat calls me; I see angels in lizards and shit in rainbows; my house in Tijuana with its evil lower rooms pulses like a small blister inside me; my father crushed and bloody; my mother dead five days undiscovered; the Sinaloa heat and my twelve-year-old fear in tropical fevers that nearly killed me, wracked with visions as I vomited all my body's waters away, and my father refusing to come near me because a Macho—a *Mexicano*—would not be so weak as to be dying of such a silly disease; the black flower of the Urreas; homeboy nephews with their sharpened screwdrivers; Jesus Christ.

I came for peace. I came to have fun. And I came to tell the tale.

Some of the writers in town seem to find my powerful reactions to them strange, I think. To them, writers are just writers. But if they had come from this desert, if they had hung on to the dream of the Word as salvation, as revenge, and justification, they might understand. These are powerful hills and powerful beasts. Medicine-women. Scorpions. Seers. I come for wisdom. I touch them and take away the slight burn of inspiration. Amen.

I come to crack that obsidian and rise.

Jesus was a walker.

Homestead Trail.

Thich Nhat Hanh tells us: "This world has many paths. Some are lined with beautiful trees, some wind around fragrant fields, some are covered with leaves and blossoms. But if we walk on them with a heavy heart, we will not appreciate them at all."

Up. Pine forests. Clearings.

I found a deer jaw, perfectly white—picked clean by critters and blanched by the elements. Another gift from the lions. Blocky teeth loose in the sockets. I put it in my pocket and charged uphill, full of life. The *L* shape of the jawbone was as cool in my shorts as a slim pistol.

It was a trip to the fair. Exciting snow patches. Tiny brooks making themselves known as they burst out from under cress leaves. A hawk. An owl turd. Field mice rolled into a furry tube decorated with a glitter of bone and nails. A tatter of lion belly-hair on a twig: yellow-cream and long, catching sun. A dandy lion tuft.

No pain.

I kept searching my body for it—frisking each muscle, limb, like a pickpocket looking for a purse. "Climb!" my body ordered. "Up!" my legs insisted. This is a direct violation of my body's usual command: "Go downhill! Lie on the couch!"

A kind of meaty joy.

Homestead Trail meets Towhee Trail up in the hills. The trail narrows, steepens, climbs along a creek until it hits Mesa Trail's access road. Suddenly, all your Dan'l Boone fantasies are dashed by a thoroughfare full of jogging great-grannies and fat guys in inappropriate shoes. But why not? The mountain wants to pull them all to its heart. And, off to the left, the Homestead itself.

First you encounter the outhouse. Vines wander in through a missing plank in the back wall. The floorboards are loose. The two-hole seat has been hungry for a pair of butts for decades and decades.

Farther up slope, the abandoned cabin. Signs ask people to please not destroy the site, and of course some dipshit has pried loose a large piece of wall to discover that the signs told the truth: there is nothing inside to steal. Except, I suppose, a little piece of the next visitor's joy.

Ghostly.

You could see, among the second- and third-growth trees, the faded lines of the old farm. Tumbledown fences suggested old stock pens, and the sketchy remains of their orchard stood like pencil drawings. But what I found most touching—and almost eerie—was a patch of tulip and lily bulbs coming up, ready to bloom.

Tilted slightly downhill, the little garden outside the cabin had run out of its bed like an escaping fishpond. It had moved downhill in an oblong flow of flowers. If you squinted, you could imagine the original neat garden. You could see the homesteader's wife planting them 100 years ago: crocus, or paperwhites. Her hands, digging in this soil. Her bent back, under this dappled light, her sack of bulbs, laying in the grand-fathers and great-grandfathers of the flowers now struggling up into the sun. Her palm, tamping the soil down. Mornings, looking for a patch of color outside the cabin door.

Eager, bright, and alone, her gesture of beauty repeated itself through time in her honor. Her desire for color, butterflies, grace, has asserted itself year after year, blessing the afternoons of hikers and wanderers who will never know her name.

Does she come here? Is she a shadow among these trees? She has left us a monument greater than any statue or head-stone. Her moment of generosity of spirit—*Give me a patch of color here*—is kind to us year after year, through the many many seasons of her absence, that green, these blossoms, her undying smile, her whisper, her hymn.

Scribes should see every mile of the Americas while there still are Americas. Every old coot dying in his Mo-Tel lobby wait-ing for a guest, every obscene redneck gas-pumper on the prai-rie, every haunted line shack and mud-bog dirt trail with a half-swallowed 3/4-ton pickup and a distraught good ol' boy in a straw cowboy hat standing in it up to his knees and saying "Gaw-*damn,*" every nice woman putting out every drooling wedge of pie on every half-dead counter in a side-road diner should be remembered. God Bless America, they used to sing, back in my old slum, the *vato* sons of lowriding *chukos* and the yellow-eyed boys of bad-ass black sports, the *pilipino* children with impeccably clean white shirts and the Irish squadron of boys all named Cherry.

I'll lay odds I'm the only one of my grade school class who made it more than a mile out of the barrio. What I never man-aged to do was move the barrio more than a mile out of me. But I've driven fast trying.

My dad had restless blood, his family surging out of some Visigoth-invaded Spanish Basquelands and spawning jovially all over Western Mexico. Ah, West: the Direction of Death in the Four Directions! Where all dead souls become cowboys and ride the skeletal horse up the nasty ridges and into the blackrock canyons! My father drove Harley and Indian motorcycles and a big black death-squad Cadillac for the President of Mexico. He grabbed the controls of a DC-3 (a C-47 to a military man) and drove that vehicle across the sky. His father hurried everywhere: hurried out of the Catholic faith, hurried into a Rosicrucian world of Mysteries, hurried North to Tijuana, hurried into a Mystical Commune, hurried back out, hurried through a clutch of children and an army of lovers, hurried to the grave. The whole lot of the Urreas talked to ghosts and saw demons and loved to drive all night.

My mother and I spent our hours trapped in the 'hood, as they call it these days; the ghetto, they used to say; *that* neighborhood. Around us, people were going crazy: Mexicans became wild and slicked their hair and dropped their cars to one inch above the road; black men jittered with nerves and anger and in spite of Dr. King shot up the walls. My dad drove all over town, making love connections and rushing away before the husbands got home. On Sundays, he'd pile us in the car and marathon-drive one, two, three hundred miles into mountains and deserts then back. All the way eating ham and cheese on sourdough and listening to "Red Roses for a Blue Lady" on the radio.

Then, *boom!* Nailed! Wabash Blvd. stop light, and a speeding woman in a big sedan: we were in our sturdy '49 Ford, and the light went green, and we started across, and she never even slowed down. She t-boned us and hurtled us across all lanes in a shower of glass and pieces of car. My mom yowling, and me lifting off the seat, levitating, floating like a feather out the shattered back window feet-first as the car spun on two-wheels, giddy sickening carnival-ride doughnuts. I can still see my feet in the blur, aiming out the port side. The old man, a cig clenched in his teeth, steered the tilting car with his left hand and reached back with the right and grabbed my collar and held me, fluttering like a flag. We didn't roll over. Crashed down in a storm of auto parts and steam. Then he let me go and I dropped back on the seat.

He told me, "Don't cry."

Years later, when I was old enough to understand, he told me, "When I become a *pendejo* behind the wheel, when I can't drive anymore, then I will die." And he did.

Morrison chants: *Ride the highway West, baby . . . The West. . . . is the best. . . .* Those big craggies—they hang up there between you and the sun—are so sharp, they *feel good,* they scrape inside your skull *real fine,* knock loose all kinds of bad memories and bus-fume crust, scrape the itchy old ugliness out. I like my skull scoured clean, scraped shiny inside as chrome. Only red miles of fossil-clogged new mountain can do that.

Exercise. Walk. Sweat.

Yesterday, I paused on a bridge to watch a trout have fun. It was in a small pool that spilled over a low wall of stones. Everything down there was emerald and gold. Water icy clear. Dapples and squiggles and colorful pebbles like a mosaic. And this fair-sized trout rode the current toward the spill backwards, leading with its tail. Then, just as it neared the spill, it gave a few lax flicks of its tail and shot back upstream, against the current. I looked down on its back and felt a surge of joy, longing. I caught myself for the first time suddenly hoping that there really might be such a thing as reincarnation. How much of heaven seemed to be there at that moment: to come back as a trout hatchling on a stream unvisited by fishermen would truly be salvation. A life beneath the rushing lens of the sky, that furling banner of blue and gray above the current. Rich colors bright with shafts of sun. Leaping into alien air to take a mayfly: diving upwards into the vertical pool of sky. Clouds of my milt moving over her roe like a submarine storm front. Then, dense and slow, sinking under the deepest cutbanks, watching the roof of the creek slow, feather over with frost, solidify and whiten. Drowse beneath winter ice. Prehistoric fish dreams shivering all up and down my slow body: the rainbows on my flanks blushing colors. This, to me, seems like all I'd need of heaven.

Sometimes, it all seems just like a poem.

Or a strange tender dream.

Writing is not strictly a process of putting words together. It is a spiritual and mental and emotional process. What we do in a literary friendship, or a romantic swoon that features copious letters, or a vibrant pen-pal relationship, is tease out the strands of each others' souls. We are tending gardens, watering plants, harvesting fruit. We are urging another side of each other's writing spirit to come out of hiding. That is feedback. That is guidance. That is editing. And that is workshopping of the highest order.

On Tour. San Antonio.

At the airport, enjoying their version of a scrambled egg break-fast. I remember how, at Harvard, we used to teach that all writing was a performance. It occurs to me this morning that all endeavors are a form of performance. If so, then cooking is like singing or writing a poem. Scrambled eggs, bacon, potato and biscuit. All over America, as the morning stripe of light moves West, skillets sing. I imagine the variations. I hear the harmonized pitch of a hundred million breakfasts.

Over by the food line, two women sit at a table and talk en-thusiastically about their cats. One of them has a bright yel-low Alpo shoulder bag decorated with a saucy portrait of Garfield. The other is slim, and her hairline is receding. She's gnawin' on a cig'ret. Apparently, her cat Chelsea is wild about Whiskas Special Blend. Chelsea got Butterfly into it, and "it started up all over again!" They think this is pretty cute, and they get a real laugh out of it.

Suddenly, the smoker leans forward and admits, "I've washed her butt in the last week."

Flying. I look down on El Paso, the southern New Mexico desert. It looks like a color photo of cells and capillaries shot through a microscope. A 3-D resonance image of a human lung. Down there, the rock is breathing.

———————

As we zero in on Las Vegas, I gaze down into the vast western emptiness. I find it strangely comforting. It scares me, too.

Dams, seen from above, reveal their drowned crags and buttes and canyons. The white flecks of boats seem to dangle just an inch above a gargantuan pre-history. It's ghostly looking down. Ghosts: the tormented skeletons of old volcanoes. The pale shades of failed roads and abandoned housing tracts, looking like they, too, had sunk beneath the surface, and the discoloration they leave on the land is the faint ripple of their passing.

Bowden says: "My home is a web of dreams. Thousands move here each year under the banners of the New West or the Sunbelt. This is the place where they hope to escape their pasts—the unemployment, the smoggy skies, dirty cities, crush of human numbers. This they cannot do. Instead, they reproduce the world they have fled. I am drawn to the frenzy of this act."

Wrecked cars tossed into the scrub. Lone tanker trucks in dismal and unforgiving dirt lots. Then, a sight I find quite astounding: a big empty dirt lot, fenced, with 100 billboards crammed inside. A cattle pen of signs! They look like they're just waiting for a cowboy to drop the cross-beams of the gate and send them stampeding—Honda, Wonder Bread, Coppertone, galloping through the city.

―――――――――

There is a crew of giddy Mexicans sitting near me. The kind who have trebly voices like saw blades, who think the more they scream, the more we'll be impressed with their sophistication. They've been sitting around Matamoros, watching gringo game shows, and they think we're all on the verge of picking the magic door and winning A BRAND-NEW CADILLAC!

Mexicali swingers.

They have come to gamble. One of them is named Juan. How do I know? He never removes his sunglasses. Or his straw cowboy hat. He is encrusted with gold: four gold chains, a gold belt-buckle, several gold rings—one of which sports a *J*. His gold bracelet reads: "JUAN." He is so pleased with himself that he has tattooed his name on his arm: *JUAN*.

The drunker they get, the louder they get. The other man in the group has hit on a joke that really works on his pals. He repeats it several times—firing on all comedy cylinders: "I brought a *TV Guide* just in case if I lose!"

Juan, overcome, throws his head back and laughs five times: Ha! Ha! Ha! Ha! *Ha!*

I suddenly suspect that to the gringos on the plane, this all must sound like the cries of some strange jungle animals: "Pooba-rooba-rooba. Ha! Ha! Ha! Ha! *Ha!*"

Juan's buddy, just as we all rise to deplane, turns to a white cowboy behind him—sporting the same straw hat that Juan is modeling—and announces: "I brought my *TV Guide* just in case I lose real early!"

The cowboy stares at him.

From the front of the plane: Ha! Ha! Ha! Ha! *Ha!*

Bitch, bitch, bitch! To wit:

Somehow, someone gave people the impression that the real world is as follows: gray; practical, which means *you must do what you don't like for reasons you don't understand but that make you feel generally bad because you're too afraid to be happy;* boring; devoid of flavor, because flavor is a wild talent, a wild gift, and the real world is covered with concrete and dictated by time cards and stop lights; the real world doesn't rhyme; the real world is a place of unspoken rules and unimagined punishments; the real world is a place where we are compelled to be miserable, and that misery we attribute to the will of God, and in doing so, we deny the fact that God made [pick any five of the following]:

geese

nipples

mud skippers

orgasms

laughter

the spleen

vulvae

boogers

sugar cane

waves

wind

volcanoes

erections

smiles

mushrooms
earthworms
armadillos
scat
columbines
quaking aspens and sacred cottonwoods
saguaros
wily coyotes
imagination; thus, poetry
somber nighthawks
stars
sweat glands
the endless symphony and banquet of smells
eggs
mates
the sound of crickets
love
death
tarantulas
and farts, which even the Pope probably finds funny.

And the "real world" seems to have all these fine things:

bills
pencils
computers
time cards
cement
cars

condoms
elevators
ulcers
migraines
pantyhose and yeast infections
alarm clocks
taxes
calculators
"day-runners"
beepers
Maalox
vibrators
Playboy
cigarettes
jackhammers
on-ramps
jock straps
parking garages
police helicopters
appointments
neckties
death squads
talk radio
nipple rings
loneliness
sunglasses
offices
fax machines
crack cocaine.

I get tired of the need we seem to have to remind ourselves that, yes, we must be *practical*. This is the *real world*. If I
were always bound to that, I'd still be with my first wife, not
writing, wearing my little tie every morning, not listening to
music, driving my Subaru through the snowstorms, burying
my nose firmly up the butts of my hideous Fascist power-mad
bosses, wearing pathetic red vest sweaters, and wondering in
the dead of night: *Is this all there is?*

I have chosen, or am choosing, against more odds than I
expected, to live beside the fresh pool of the heart's sweet water. I used to live in those smoky towers over there. See them?
The bullets ping off the steel walls of the buildings, and the
small fires ignited by everyone's crashing hopes burn orange
in the alleys. And I'd hide behind the curtain and peek off at
the lavender-hued sunset. I knew the pool was out there. I
knew deer sipped at its edge. And I knew those mad ones had
gone there, and some had prospered and some had died in the
woods, lost: Kerouac, Mary Oliver, Ed Abbey, Tom McGuane,
Annie Dillard, Thoreau, Gabriel García Márquez, Jimi
Hendrix, Rosario Castellanos, Basho, John the Baptist, Joan
of Arc, and Neruda, Neruda, forever Neruda!

Teresita.

So, around 1990, I started to walk. I started to hike out of
there. It was hard, don't get me wrong: my mother was the
first sacrifice, and the journey began with her small box of
ashes—like I said in *Fever of Being,* ashes that looked like five
pounds of seashells—leaping out of my hands into the rushing waves of the Sound, at the tip of Cape May, New Jersey.
Cascades of storm light falling out of immense clouds, and a

white heron standing in the marsh at my back, gleaming like a searchlight. Down the beach, haunted gun emplacements, left behind by my mother's beloved World War II soldiers, and now inhabited by eerie whispers and scuttling crabs.

I lost my job, lost every cent. Drove across the USA in that dying Subaru and that dying marriage. Went to South Dakota and sweated in the Oglala way hunched in a lodge. Started fixing up my family home. Started writing for the *Reader*. Left for Boulder.

This is the real world, you see. This. This heat. These words. These feelings. This magic. This love which I cannot contain. Yes, these troubles. But this glory, this hope, this work, these days, these hikes, this desire, these smoky erotic nights, this expectation, this literature, this landscape, these publications, these friends, this blaring music, these movies, this house. This journal. This small, yet growing, feeling of hope.

I am in the real world, but I'm crouched at the shore of that sweet pool I longed for. I am sad to see there are still troubles at the pool, but how could there not be? Yes, deer sip from it, but there are lions waiting to eat them. That's the way things are.

I have often told about the strange experience I had at the top of the Hyatt or whatever it is beside the San Diego seaport. I was on tour, and they put me in a suite on the 25th floor: it had all kinds of cool stuff, like French doors between the various rooms, and a bar, and all kinds of let's-turn-this-guy-into-a-hippo snacks. And one wall, beside my bed, was glass. And the window looked south. And I wasn't thinking about much, just cruising around before the window naked, pleased to be waggling my various body parts at all of Coronado and the San Diego harbor, when I looked out at the lights of ... Tijuana. Tijuana, sitting there like a frost of gems on mounds of black velvet, all those faint lights glittering. And I froze. For there, in the middle of the TJ sprawl, was my old hill. Was my old house. Was my old history. Was my old garden, with its giant pill-bugs and giant ants, its dusty dogs and its old banana trees and its pomegranate tree. I knew, exactly, where my old tormented and charmed infancy lay among those earth-bound traffic-light stars.

I sat on the bed and stared. And, just this side of TJ, burned the sad lights of National City. The dull glow of 420 W. 20th St., the last lights of my godparents' home and the fragile hope and beauty I found there. The fabric of ashes that seems to hold me together through everything—the strange and exotic taste of family love.

And, yes, closer still, and to the east, the tainted lights of Logan Heights. Crack addicts shooting it out with *cholos* on National Avenue, the ghosts of my terror and despair still there. The shadow of that lonely little boy still crouching beneath the tattered old hibiscus bushes, clutching his plastic gun.

It was all there, before me, my impossible, impoverished past.

And here I was, on the 25th floor of some mad hotel, in a room that cost more for one night than I used to earn in a month. Sitting on a bed. Unimaginable air conditioning cooling my pampered skin. Some sort of fizzy European fruit-flavored water giggling in my gut. And books, *books by me,* on the bookshelves all over America.

I used to be down there, looking up. And now, here I was, like a king in a mythical tower, looking down. Wondering: How did I get here?

And: Why?

I crouch at the pool now, looking back upon the burning falsehood of the "real world."

I have committed to a soulful life, and I have walked awfully far to get here—so far that I have begun to speak a new language. Is it any wonder that my beloved, my family, and even my friends, don't always understand me? Writers have always been aliens. How doubly alien, then, to come out of the woods like Johnny Appleseed. I have twigs in my hair and birds on my shoulders. I know it.

Their children understand. They and the dogs. They live at the pool's edge; we're neighbors. A little girl who cannot read somehow already knows the story.

All the teachers, priests, psychologists, nuns, textbooks, tests, rulers, and television shows are already trying to pull her away. The dog will stay here, but the little girl will be lured into the city. She'll look back for a few years, remember how the birds flew here, but she'll be clothed in gray soon and shuttled onto the People-Mover, cables slotted into her head, and a mainframe switch-box attached to her heart.

We write to drop feathers into the machine.

Just remember: poems, moonlight, cottonwoods, wells. Blue.
Red. Aspens . . . doesn't that word just lull you to sleep? . . .
aspens . . . it sounds like the wind moving down the side of the
mountains, blowing all my bad dreams away . . . moving the
fog out over the plains . . . all the colors so tender you can
almost taste them: aspens . . . aspens . . . aspens. . . .

Summer

I grasp
in the darkness of the heart
a firefly.

—*Buson*

Have you ever seen a mirage? I never saw one. At least not one of those visions you read about in books or see in movies. No city of gold, no Arab towers floating in the air, no phantom ocean in the middle of the badlands. The closest I've come to seeing a real mirage is those pools of silver air on the highway, about half-way to the horizon. They look like mirrors, not water. Maybe liquid metal, like mercury. And when the big trucks come toward you, cutting across the desert on their way to Texas and Oklahoma, then it starts to look like a vision of some kind. The trucks start out invisible, then wobble up out of the shining air-pools, like they were melting in reverse, like an ice cube pulling itself together from a steamy puddle, only these ice cubes are painted candyapple red or metalflake blue and have chrome brows and weigh about a million tons. Rising, like a vision, like a dream, like a new poem, wobbly as hatchlings, growing just like words from the black heat of the earth.

Colorado. Friday. A memory.

Sitting at Tom Horn's grave. Me and all the other dead men taking our afternoon leisure.

My wife behind in her suffering, weeping on the porch. The agony of a wife. My mistake. But we both must pay.

So I sit by the grave of the "exterminator." His rosy head-stone reads: "IN LOVING MEMORY OF TOM HORN 1861–1903." You see, somebody loved the killer, even after he himself was killed. Maybe in this world someone will love us.

Nearby, in this boneyard, someone plucks a banjo. It's

weird, a sound Tom himself would recognize, some settler's ghost working through the scales with the tireless 19th-century banjo sound. Tom Horn's toebones slowly beginning to tap. He's smiling. The dead are always happy—just look at how their skulls keep grinning.

Tom Horn knew how to kill; if only I could learn how to live.

I long now for Spanish in my bed. I long for the understanding of *frijoles, tortillas, el cucuy*. If I heard the tone of voice a Mexican woman uses to soothe away pain, I would openly weep. I would follow her. I would climb into her smell. But that road is not open today.

I am losing myself.

I drip away like blood from a gun shot.

I dream in Spanish.

I am having trouble hearing white voices.

That's why I talk to Tom Horn. He speaks Apache. He speaks Mexican. I come to beg him to arm himself, to rise, horribly rise, ride this relentless night, take aim, draw a bead, and slaughter these 100 dead shadows who oppress me.

Tom Horn—please kill these ghosts.

Rock Springs, Wyoming: Heading West.

I'm camping in the Outer Ring of Hell KOA. Industrial Kamping. That's no joke—it's a bare patch of gravel hidden from the freeway by a row of oil tanks. A beautiful young blond woman makes camp three feet away from me and she stares at me as if asking, *What are we doing here?*

I drove helplessly, circling Rock Springs looking for a) a book store, b) a bank, and c) anything at all of interest. Oil riggers stood in the weedy courtyards of duplex settlements and offered to kick my ass if I cared to pull over. Large dark women held children by one arm and stared down from the balconies of weekly-rate motels. I drove past the same hooker three times. She was sitting on a curb down by the tracks in shorts and a sweet flowery blouse. She had the blues, but she sat up straight and put on her game face when I drove by. The second time I passed, she seemed sure she was going to make $15. By the third pass, she knew I was just lost. Back to the blues, head on knees, elaborately painted eyes drifting to I-80. Who knows how many miles she drove that day. All the way to the ocean, all the way to Katmandu.

I ended up parked on the street between a bar and a porn shop. The men in the bar were shouting. A guy in front with an oil-slick tan regarded me and my Colorado plates and looked like someone had just passed gas in his face and stepped into the bar. "Hey boys," I could imagine him saying. "Check out the dipshit that just pulled up." In my mind, the biggest Hells Angel in there was saying, "By Jove, I do believe this chappie is a poet. Shall we thrash him within an inch of his life, my good men?" And the various bikers, gunslingers, cannibals, and highwaymen all shouted, "What ho! The game is afoot! Tally-ho, ye Bounders!"

I beat it into the porn shop.

Besides, I was so bored, I needed a shock. Not too shocking. Counters with big rubber items. Deflated nude women with air nozzles in their butts. The following titles were in evidence (and me standing there jotting in my notebook while smelly men moved away from me like I was a pervert): Pink Passion, Jenny's Anal Encounter, Big Boobies, Blubber Buns, Finger Friggin! and Let's Play Lez.

One hilarious note: the vile pornhouse operator was busily studying *Wheel of Fortune* on a tiny black-and-white television. Pat Sajak's avaricious commentary was not entirely out of place amid the collected latex.

I abandoned the town to certain nuclear annihilation and drove out into the deserted landscape. God was doing some really good stuff with the sunset and the clouds, but I still felt too profaned to look closely. It felt like I had to let the sad faces and the sadder anatomies drain out of my eyes before I could see anything.

I pulled a U-turn in the middle of a road that went empty into either horizon. Just stopped in the middle of it and let the parched wind rock the Jeep. I could have slept right there in the southbound lane. Drove back to camp and took a shower. The blond was zipped in, her shadow on the tent wall hunched over a book. I wanted it to be one of mine. Clouds put down spider-legs of lightning and minced along the hills.

The Sticker Says: *Big Wonderful Wyoming.*

All kinds of strange Wyoming jokes. Somebody thought "Wyoming" sounded like a verb: "Mom! Junior's wyoming again!"

Strange Beautiful: Flaming Gorge, Utah.

"Soon enough," Jimi Hendrix sings, "time will tell / About the surface of the wishing well. . . . " "The Burning of the Midnight Lamp," perhaps his loneliest song, perhaps *the* loneliest song. Jimi's pain and fear hidden in waves of electric sky-church sound, hidden by our own deafness to his voice. I drive my Jeep up the psychedelic rocks above Flaming Gorge. Park on a peak—edge of the world.

His voice sails from the speakers, catches updrafts and tilts toward heaven with the eerie cry of a redtail hawk; black diamond sparkles on raven wings. Visions of Jimi in my head: hunched over the notebook, writing those words as the dark jet carries him over the black sea, to England, to his fate. What will become of him? Will anyone hear his music? Everyone around him is asleep, and he sighs, and he writes: "Loneliness is such a drag." Can you see his eyes as they close? Dream on, Jimi. Dream on.

I drive down into Flaming Gorge still listening. Fossils all around me in the brightly hued cliffs, and Jimi's music now a fossil itself. All of Jimi's heart and terror and rage and hope burned through his guitar, and the feedback doubled back and took him away. Jimi's gone on the wings of a dragonfly. Other substances have seeped into his songs now. All our myths and legends and prejudice and need, and they have filled the spaces between the notes and hardened there and turned the music into a gem. These facets reflect ourselves to ourselves.

The tape rolls on as I sink through geologic time. "Third Stone from the Sun" still trying to show me the world where

I move so blindly: Jimi's soaring, melting, burning, storming guitar is the exact portrait of this landscape: black spaceship clouds crawl on lightning legs across screaming stone.

I had a dream: a small store around the corner. In a glass cabinet, three small flames bright on small white stones. "These," the owner whispered, "are the last flames left from Monterey. He burned his guitar at Monterey." I bought one flame, carried it out in a jade box.

Somewhere in the desert I put the flame to my tongue, lay back and waited. He came to me. Walking through the stars.

I awake to a morning—golden rose. Wherever I go, I know he's gone there too. In midnight terror, his fear has been there too. His loneliness, laughter, dreamtime and sorrow. He's far before me, walking too.

The breeze comes rippling off the lake.

I throw a rock full of fossils in the back of the Jeep. The map is wet: *still raining . . . still dreaming.* How can you love a soul through a few electric notes?

I drive down the crimson gorge. *Dear Jimi,* I think, *the wind really does cry Mary.*

Crow Agency, Montana.

A Crow Indian evangelist sat with me while I ate Indian Tacos out of the back of a beat-up van. His business card said: "Evangelist Harold Ennick, Crow Agency Montana." And: "With

God All Things Are Possible Matthew 19:26." And: "*Jesus* is the Answer!" And: "*Jesus* is Worthy to be Praised! (Revelation 5:12)." It was an informative card.

On the side of the van, a hand-lettered sign:

ONCE YOU TRY OUR INDIAN TACO'S

YOU'LL KNOW THE MEANING OF

GOOD.

They were right.

Nearby, the bingo hall was called REZ-A-VEGAS.

Brother Ennick told me, "The old Indian ways are Satanic."

A visiting Apache preacher, Mr. Stanley Kill, sat in a plastic-mesh lawn chair in a shady spot under a cottonwood and laughed at almost everything. He was happy about the day, the fry bread, the imminent tent revival, and about my shorts.

"Lot of pockets," he noted.

"How's that taco?" Brother Kill asked.

"Good!" I said.

This, too, made him laugh.

Brother Ennick asked me for my address so we could write to each other. I reached in my pocket for a pen, but the road being what it is, I pulled out a little tube of Aquafresh toothpaste instead. I thought Brother Kill was going to pass out from laughing at that one. Brother Ennick laughed, the women in the taco van laughed, I laughed. Everybody standing around laughing at a tube of toothpaste.

As I was getting ready to leave, Brother Ennick confided the strangest thing to me. I don't know what kind of mystery he was trying to share, but after he was through saying it, he said, "It's true!"

And Brother Kill simply nodded.

What Brother Ennick told me was: "They tell us not to be prejudiced, but they got prejudiced machines."

Tongue River.

On to the Little Bighorn: 100 Hells Angels milling among the restless spirits; Crazy Horse still riding up the fateful ravine. Everywhere, searching for the shadows of Brother Ennick's machines.

Walked up to the haunted hilltop. Various rangers and Indians gave talks. It was eerie to be in that ghost-field—I could imagine the cries and the gunfire so vividly, the roar and choke of smoke and dust. People scattered over the golden ridges bowed their heads and seemed to say small prayers to Jehovah and Tunkasila.

Of course, on these hills, Reno and Custer and Benteen were also calling to the One Above, but He seemed to be listening to only one side that day.

Many bikers had gathered in their black T-shirts and black engineer boots, black leather vests and black leather leggings, black leather coats, black dusters, black jeans, black gloves.

Both outlaws and jovial AMA riders on chrome-dripping hogs. Later in the day, at the Little Blackfoot, one of them with a FUCK EVERYTHING black T-shirt would pass by, show me an AA "One Day At A Time" sticker on his chain guard, and give me the thumbs-up as he charged into the distance. The Hells Angels' ambassador of good will and serenity.

I stood looking into this dead man's hillside, and all these motorized long riders circled the battlefield disconsolately on their deep-voiced iron horses. They haggled with the Crow women selling trinkets along the roadway.

Crazy Horse, the ranger said, rode up that gully there, coming out here on this side of the hill.

Crazy Horse!

There. Up the gully. It struck fear into me even after a hundred years.

I walked to Custer's death-marker. Strange feelings were in my heart—a bit of joy, I must admit. But it's a sad place. A strange and intense place.

Now we head back down the hill.

Leave the ghosts to fight the wind and silence.

Timeless sorrow

and peace.

And:

The Bighorn River.
Two Leggins Canal.
Pryor Creek.
The Yellowstone.

Boulder River.
The Gallatin.

Best Place Name In the United States:
What Cheer, Iowa.

Crossing the Soldier River.
The Little Sioux River.
Suddenly, I am in love with rivers, I want to collect them, their names, the long line of poetry they etch all across the American page. I pluck up the letters of their names and then like fossils I drop them into the big pockets of my army pants.
Beaver Creek.
The East Vermillion.
The West Vermillion.
Wolf Creek.

Saddest sight of the night: a little dog running panicked beside the freeway in the immense darkness outside of Sioux Falls.

Mitchell, South Dakota. Morning, July 28.

Here to see the amazing, goofy and majestic Corn Palace. Every year, someone builds a palace out of corn. It's delightful. You can smell the walls of the building from the street. It's the only building I ever visited that smelled like a field. Tourists as awestruck as I wander by, staring up, saying, "Made *entirely* out of *corn!*"

Great Plains winds buffet the town, slivers of Corn Palace peeling loose and spiraling away. Paper cups catch a gust and skitter and rattle away in skipping loops. Bikers everywhere, on their way to the Black Hills for the Sturgis rally.

Other sights of note in Mitchell: a giant plastic bull, a giant jackalope, a giant white bigfoot.

The Big Mo.

The Mad River.

Re-crossing the Missouri at Pierre.

McGuane says: "The average American is 2/3 river water. . . ." I like to ask my students: What body of water makes up 2/3 of you?

Driving on the Great Plains: you could see so far that storms in the next state were small columns of shadow. We all drove 75, 80, 85. Power line towers receded in the distance, in each direction, till they grew small and vanished over the curve of the earth.

White River.

Little White River.

Cheyenne River.

Belle Fourche River.

The Mad Horse River.

Dead Horse Creek.
The Powder River.
Goose Creek.
Crazy Woman Creek.

God.

It was in Santa Fe. I heard this guy talking about God. This is what he said:

"They's just two things you need to know about God. One: they is one. Two: you ain't it."

Benson, Arizona, 1988:
The Chief's 4 Feathers Kampground.
Your Hosts: Bill & Bert!

The Chief (Bill!) drives a golf cart from campsite to campsite, delivering burgers, ranch beans, and baked potatoes. Last night, we sat on the Chief's picnic table and watched Benson's 4th of July Celebration. About ten fireworks popped into the sky, and cowboys honked their horns. Then, everybody drove away. I wandered over to the lighted pool, wobbling away like electric Jell-O, and watched a skinny male tarantula scoot around the rim with his butt raised anxiously.

This morning, I had the urge to see vinegarroons, bobcats, coyotes. Chuckwallas and coatimundis. We headed back to Tucson and visited the Desert Museum. But when we got out to the parking lot at the end of the day, the Jeep had a stroke. I tried to start it, and it wheezed miserably, then coughed, then just choked and burped black puffs of smoke.

Forty minutes later, a Chevy tow truck appeared. Our Hero leaped out: a big young 'un with a moustache and stubble. His open shirt revealed an expanse of colorfully sunburned gut. Black flecks of Copenhagen chaw stuck to his teeth. He spit a concentrated stream, straight as a laser. His CB handle: BRAVO.

Bravo's first act, after he looked under the Jeep, was to invite us home with him.

"Spend the night. I got seven rooms. Got a spare bedroom with a bed and a couch. It's not fancy, but it's a house."

My wife, given to seeing the worst in strange men, and fearing some sort of cannibalistic Satanic desert death cult, shook her head at me every time Bravo looked away.

"Uh, I guess not," I said.

Bravo was disappointed, but not hurt. He put his hook through the lip of the Jeep and lifted it. Yanked out a hunk of our drive train and tossed it into the back of his truck. Then he pulled us onto the highway, and struck an instant deal: "I'll haul you forty miles for $90."

"Deal."

On the road, Bravo revealed myriad incredible details of his life. He also demonstrated a real Old West country-boy genius for bullshit.

Examples:

Ohio's dreaded "Blue Hole"—right near Yellow Springs—a bottomless pit filled with water. "They dropped lead weights in there, and they just kept on going. Never hit bottom." It seems this one feller with a horse team and a wagon started out to cross it and sank. Bravo reported, with some dread, "They say he came up in New Hampshire. Them horses was still in their traces. . . ."

Also, there was the revelation that dam divers, who swim down dam faces inspecting for cracks, periodically find *monster fish*. "One guy I know got down there and ran into a catfish fourteen foot long!"

As if that weren't enough: "One time I was fishing bass out of that same dam. This guy pulls up in a truck. He has a tow cable hooked up to a winch. He takes a big steel meat hook, puts a pot roast on it, reels out the cable and drives the truck away. He pulls out a six-foot fish!"

Bravo has apparently eaten every mammal on the continent: he offered us detailed gastronomic reviews of the merits of munching javelina, squirrel, coon, skunk, possum. Deer and rabbit are almost too mundane for Bravo to pass judgment on. Pit-barbecuing a wild boar, however, is the ultimate mammal-chomp experience.

"After about twelve hour, you can take you a butter-knife and cut off a slab!"

Bravo was discharged from the Navy after punching out his CPO.

"I don't have a good relationship with authority."

Bravo had just received a Dear John letter. His wife was leaving him for an Air Force guy he'd once thrown in a duck pond. First the Air Force fight, then the Dear John letter, then the CPO fight—Bravo's tenure in the Armed Forces was just about up.

After he had thrown the jet jockey in the pond, Bravo went to his truck, the truck being some sort of neutral territory. But the guy came out of the duck pond, clearly looking for more trouble. "And one thing I had plenty of was *trouble!*" So one thing led to another, and Bravo threw a punch.

"He covered up like a boxer. I hit his arm, broke both bones. Snap!" (My wife, crammed in the cab with Bravo and me, was squirming.) "My next punch broke his jaw in three places. Guess I was a little upset. I went to the door and told my wife, `You better come collect your boyfriend. He's laying out in the street holding up traffic.'"

This is a classic Bravo *bon mot*.

It turns out that a variation had served him well earlier. When he threw the flyboy in the pond, he went to her door and said, "You better come out here and collect your boyfriend. He's gettin' all wet."

Git 'em, Bravo!

Bravo also enjoyed adventures in Tijuana.

"Hangin' out with a bunch of nice-lookin' seen-your-reeters."

He was with a Cajun boy named Billy Bob. Enraged Mexican boyfriends were easily lifted with one fist. Their shirt collars acted as handles. These Mexicans were, to a man, "sent flying."

I learned the astonishing fact that Mexicans tear open their own clothes. It's a sign of grief.

On the road between Tucson and Benson, Bravo's tow truck broke down three times. He radioed all over the state to bitch about it. His wife and kids left him and moved to Germany. His father was back at the seven-room house dying of emphysema. When Bravo finally got us back to the 4 Feathers, he shook my hand, then drove away with my drive train still rattling in the back of his truck.

Excellent road sign outside of Phoenix, AZ:

UTOPIA CLOSED.

Home.

Today I was visited by a most peculiar insect. I was in the back yard wandering with the dog, feeling as American as I possibly could. When out of the tomato patch, this whirling flying dervish came bombing through the trees and did high-speed loops around me. It was about the size of a cicada.

Zoom!

And then it was gone.

Boink!

It was back!

Zip!

Gone again!

Hello, here I am!

Oops! Gotta go!

Zoom!

Suddenly, I realized it was on my back, and when I turned to look, it shot off again. Then, like magic, it materialized for an instant on the leg of my shorts. In that brief moment, I was startled to see it was a butterfly. It had the amusing and jaunty shape of a skipper, only bigger. The undersides of its wings were unremarkable mottled charcoal. But the topsides were black with a bright line of colored spots along the edge, and . . . *Zoom!*

Its maneuvers looked like what might happen if you fed a bat diet pills.

Another one appeared, and they did a fierce dogfight all over the yard. But, apparently fascinated by my shorts, the attacker repeatedly broke off the assault and buzz-bombed me, hitting and plucking off the fabric in the briefest landings.

Dear boy, I'd love to stay, but I simply *must* fly over there and kick the ass of that dreadful interloper.

Zoom!

Rosario Castellanos wrote:

Only silence is wise.

But I am constructing, as if with a hundred bees,
one small hive with my words.

Reading *Lady Faustus.*

Aside from my general crush on her, I'm sure my response to Diane Ackerman's work is erotic. My response to most writing probably has some essence of eros—after all, I take it into my bed, I hold it close to my heart, I pull it into myself and bear it inside my head and chest like a small red thing, then I roll phrases from it around on my tongue. I feel an equally erotic throb for the land when I'm up on the Rockies, panting, heart pounding, sweat tickling its way down my spine, spicy scents in my nose and salt on my tongue. And I lie back on the mountain in the heat, and I feel her breathing beneath me. That's a good time to crack open a Diane Ackerman book.

She's one of those writing heroes who changed my life in a very particular way. I remember first stumbling upon her long essay on "Bats" in the *New Yorker.* It was like a punch—no kidding. I dragged it around for weeks, making people read it. It immediately formed a mini-anthology in my mind with Chuck Bowden's amazing bat cave chapter in *Blue Desert.* This two-essay anthology was a best-seller in my skull. I proudly announced to my friends that I had the two best bat stories ever published in my possession, as if I myself had somehow not only written them both, but had constructed Chuck and Diane from some model kit. (Mattel's BRILLIANT WRITER KIT! *Almost Lifelike.* Insert tab A into slot B. Glue not included.)

Of course, nobody cared about bats.

But it hit some others over the head, too—Lowry Pei joined some sort of bat society after reading the piece. Bats! I LOVED BATS! ACKERMAN DROVE ME BATTY FOR BATS. What a great gift. Bats, of course, are better than any piece of writing: I'd rather burn a book than a bat. They also wipe out more mosquitoes in one night than even an old blood-smeared and tattered impromptu flyswatter like the silver foil paperback edition of *The Shining* could nail in a year.

Aside from all that, however, there is the very sexy power of Ackerman's boldness, her words, and her freedom. And there is my personal delight in woman-warriors. How exciting it is to know a fierce woman. She strides into the world, armed and dangerously alive.

Go, sister. More power, more power to you.

At the zoo. A black-leather white biker couple strolled along with us. She was chunky, blond, with a foxtail peeking out from under the hem of her coat. He was the archetypal skinny biker you see riding by—long dark hair, craggy cheeks, maybe a tooth missing, and the guys call him "Buzzard" or "Philthy Phil." Little squished leather bomber-pilot cap on his head, beard, at least 10 earrings in his ears. His hands were purple with tattoos. Hanging from his belt: a pewter KKK medallion. Hanging down the front of his pants, off his chained-on keys, a steel swastika.

They liked the African lions.

She had one of those cardboard Kodaks.

"Look at them *lahns,*" he said.

She eagerly snapped a picture.

A nice day at the zoo with the Nazis.

No matter what instant liberal thing I could say or think about them, *they were at the zoo, eating Eskimo pies and loving the lahns.* They probably called each other "honey" and "baby" and had to pay bills. Had favorite songs. Had moms. Believed in things that I probably believed in, too.

Who was this man, really? What could his life possibly be like? Maybe I should have just asked him.

Thunder coming. I can hear it grumbling beyond the peaks. Clouds lift their heads over the Flatirons—Devil's Thumb is poking them in the chin as they peek down at us. *Get ready,* they whisper. *We're comin' to get ya!*

August, Around My Birthday.

Birthday, yeah, okay—but let's get to something more important: News of the Rockies.

It's been raining and the creeks are going crazy, trying to wrestle with cars on the freeways. Greatly in evidence along my daily hike is Boulder Creek, alive with little rapids and mini-waterfalls and trout and anonymous fish. The whole path is shaded by trees: apple, plum, aspen, willow, some sort of maple, three kinds of pine, blue spruce, and holy cottonwoods. I have learned from our Indian friends an unreasonable romantic approach to a cottonwood.

Dennis Martinez, brilliant Pima restoration ecologist, startled me the other day by vanishing as we walked through town. I turned back and found him with his arms around an ancient cottonwood. He was holding it as tenderly as a lover, murmuring something into its bark. Boy, the rednecks would love this: a real tree-hugger! Something very clean and precious came clear to me in that moment, though. You couldn't be tougher, or stronger, or more fierce than Dennis. And you'd have to be that strong in yourself to go out into the world and embrace what you love. *Embrace it,* just once, and tell it you love it. Who has the guts to do it? Watching Dennis, loving him and the tree wildly, I also thought: who would dare make fun of this man? With his red bandanna and his eagle eyes, they'd be afraid to lose their teeth.

Real Men Hug Trees.

And Dennis told me: "You always know a cottonwood because its leaves look like hearts the size of hands waving at you."

The mountain has taught me much this year, as I have fed it my drops of sweat. Bishop Poma, of the Aimara, took me aside and told me that in Bolivia, the Indians call the earth La Pachamama. Each drink or meal must be tasted first by her. Holy Communion is always done in the native villages in this way: La Pachamama takes the first sip of wine. They splash it on the ground. Fundamentalists find this practice pagan and barbaric; the natives find the fundamentalists rude and disrespectful. I'm with Bishop Poma as I splash small sips of myself onto La Pachamama's understanding lips. I suppose it's a communion all its own, in its many definitions.

Drops of sweat, drops of ink, happy tears.

Blake once said: "No person who is not an artist can be a Christian."

I'm thinkin' about this when I climb.

Many of the mountain's lessons are directly related to writing, having as they do, an almost religious depth. For example: I was suddenly overcome with sorrow when I realized that I walked the peaks every day and knew not a thing about the plants all around me. It was bad enough that I didn't know what the flowers were, but how could I make believe I was a mountain man and not know what the edible plants were? I couldn't eat a doggone thing.

In writing, I come across a similar blindness. I suddenly realize I don't know how to achieve a certain effect, or scene. And suddenly it appears. It was always there; I just couldn't see it.

That same day, on my hike, I discovered two different kinds of plums, grapes, berries, apples, sweet peas. They were there all along, of course. But I wanted to see them, and they showed themselves. Pay attention—that is the law. I've been sampling the Rockies' salad bar ever since.

I can't even say what the cottonwoods have shown me about writing. Maybe it's grace, maybe it's effortlessness. For example, there is an old grandfather cottonwood (*alamo* in Spanish) between my house and the Flatirons. I sit on my porch and watch it, and those heart-shaped leaves start to wave. But the most amazing thing happens. The leaves pick up the light and throw it back. They reflect the light and transform into ten thousand small mirrors: the whole tree lights up and starts to throw sparks, looks like a giant Christmas tree decorated with flashbulbs. All this excitement from dull green leaves and a breeze. What simple power to transfix. I'd like to write exactly like that tree glistens.

Walking = Writing.

The other night, when I wanted to dream of you and failed, but woke up somehow with you, I wanted to read you my favorite poem. I wanted to hover near your ear, float there and move your hair aside, and whisper verses to you. I love so many poems, I don't know if I could pick out *the* favorite. I especially love one, though. The first time I read it, I actually sighed. I put the book down and felt healed. It's by Wendell Berry, our mad farmer (he knows the soil, the pulse of Our Mother, the flutter of the holy leaves). And, interestingly enough, it's called "Envoy," which is what I'd be on that night floating by your pillow: your special envoy from the Other World, that beautiful place we walk to when the mail comes. So I would have read you this poem in the dream, and I would have whispered this poem to you in your sleep, and I offer it to you now on the snowfield of this page:

> Love, all day there has been at the edge of my mind
> the wish that my life would hurry on,
> my days pass quickly and be done,
> for I felt myself a man carrying a loose tottering
> bundle along a narrow scaffold: if I could carry it
> fast enough, I could hold it together to the end.
>
> Now, leaving my perplexity and haste,
> I come within the boundaries of your life, an interior
> clear and calm. You could not admit me burdened.

I approach you clean as a child of all that has been
with me.
You speak to me in the dark tongue of my joy
that you do not know. In you I know
the deep leisure of the filling moon. May I live long.

It's a perfect friend-poem. Or a love-poem. Or lover-poem.
Or marriage-poem. If I could write a poem as beautiful as
that, I'd sleep well for one night.

And if I could whisper to you, I'd lay it by your ear like a
pearl.

Sunrise, 9/15.

Outside my window, a small valley, still full of shadow, like a
nocturnal flood slowly draining away. To the west, a tall cottonwood, alive in every section with wind. Once you know
who the trees are, you get to see how each one responds to the
world, the day. They each seem to have personalities, or should
I coin a new phrase? Arboralities, perhaps? Anyway, distinct
presences. The stolid, faithful evergreens. The flouncy, excit-
able fruit trees. The optimistic cottonwoods. Unfortunately, I
still know so few of them. I'm trying to learn, trying to know
them all. Lately, I've been looking at mesquites, trying to get
an angle on the oaks. I haven't yet gotten a feel for them.

I must invite one over for tea.

fall

Three times it cried out
but now not heard anymore,
a deer in the rain.
—*Buson*

Astounding light falling sideways onto the ground. Aspens, our little friends, quivering silver—a rainstorm of quarters.

Fall comes down the Rockies in a mantle of fog, cold breath, and rumbling. The Flatirons have disappeared from my window. Water is running in the air like an invisible wafer—horizontal between us and Glenwood Springs. Or arcing, forming a vast cup and touching down on either side of the mountains.

I almost grabbed a black widow today. She'd come into the kitchen to escape the cold. She was going down the wall next to the sink on one silk wire and I reached over to grab her and toss her out, when for some reason I stopped just as my hand closed on her. Caught her in a glass and stared at the red hourglass on her belly.

Peter Michelson came over, peered in at her, and said, "No mercy for the spider!"

She was elegant in the glass. I wished her well, apologized, and said a small sort of benediction over her: something about delicious fat roaches in the sewers. Then I flushed her down the toilet. She clenched her legs to herself and body-surfed the maelstrom all the way down.

Boulder Creek Canyon.

Maniac rock climbers across the creek are splayed on the walls like colorful bugs. Magnificence everywhere. The climbers' colors in the fall sun are flavorful against the rock.

Elsewhere in the Boulder Creek News: a tree trunk has made its way down the Front Range, on its journey to the South Platte and the high plains. It has come to rest here, at my own resting place. Stripped of branches and bark, and buffed, planed and sanded by its journey, it's as sleek as a base-ball bat. It lies in icy water waiting for the next flood to move it down to the small rapids as the creek turns to cut through Boulder. There, it might make a small dam for a while. It might even freeze in place, ice gluing it to the rocks where eddies are mild enough. Small bass and trout might creep into its shadow and grow dense and slumber through the winter. But spring is surely coming, and when the melt and runoff hit, the whole thing will be resting outside the Boulder library. A new condo for literary fish.

It's funny how a place, in this case a trail, becomes your companion. How spots all along it become familiar, then be-come friends. As though the footpath were a live thing. From the parking lots in town, to the cliffs at Elephant Rock or Lover's Leap, to the oaks and the pines, the bridges, the small waterfalls. I love them all, and I enjoy sharing them. Every-one who comes here is a generous lover. And the mountain knows it's always our birthday when we come, and it offers us each a brightly wrapped gift. Bright as foil paper. These gifts are personal, and hard to explain.

For example, how would I describe the fluttering dappled surface of this page as I write? If I wanted to tell my distant friends about it, I would have to bring them to this flat rock, on this day, at this time of the afternoon. They probably should be tired. I'd have to open a book to a blank page, wait for a cloud to pass, a beam of autumn sun to slant down through the leaves, and a breeze to set those leaves dancing so their color smears across the sunbeam as their shadows interrupt it. Then I could say: "Behold."

The page itself comes alive. The constant *Sss* of the water sounds like the paper is singing. How can you write that?

Today, Linda Hogan said: "Poetry is an act of caring." And then she said: "The body is a sovereign nation." Every mile up the mountain, my bones say: God bless Linda Hogan.

Evangelist at the Dalton Trumbo Fountain at CU: "Their God is their penis!" Later: "Whores, whoremongers, and masturbators!" He yells, his voice rising like heat waves before the glacier high up in the mountains. Oddly obsessed, the guy has a real thing about those whores and those wankers: "You don't have to be a sexual pervert! All you have to do is *want* to be one! And you *are*!" Then: "Christian masturbators!" And: "Become a slave to the living God! You have the choice today!" He also called us sexual perverts (again), adulterers, drunks, sodomizers, queers. And he has the gall to shout at us about *Love*. Love! How dare he.

These sidewalk preachers remind me of men in a car who pull up to a woman and wolf-whistle and scream and bark and pound on the car doors. What do they think? That the woman will swoon, overcome with love? Fools. Masturbators, indeed.

Love? What portrait of Christ do these semiliterate backwoods rubes think they are painting? He cries: "Are you a Christian or do you just get up on Saturday mornings and watch TV?" (Eh?) And: "We got queer churches!" And: "We got masturbators and the Church is counseling them to do it!" And the Catholics "take a cookie and think they can change it into the body of Christ!" And: "Porty! Porty! Porty! And next week you gotta go out and dew it agin! Porty! Porty! Porty!"

Every time he says *Jesus,* every time he says *Christ,* every time he says *Christian,* every time he says *Bible* . . . every time he says the Pope *is gonna burn,* the Catholics *are gonna burn,* Buddhists *are gonna burn,* the Virgin Mary is *an unvirginal woman,* more and more students flee. One by one, lashed by the warty angry red tongue of American Xianity, they flee.

"My own mother is an alcoholic!" he cries.

There's his answer. He needs Al-Anon.

Then he needs a hearty wank with a handful of Jell-O.

Supper last night with Lorna Dee Cervantes and Jay Griswold. That mad ranger poet *pistolero* and I hunched in the corner like two Boy Scouts with a *Playboy.* Lorna's salsa music poured over our heads as we muttered passionately about the joy in the objects of the world, the raw poems of things. Every once in a while, one of us would say something that would make us fall silent and squint, as if we could see through walls. Bird dogs, for example. Four-wheel drive, Lorca, haiku, a twelve-gauge pump loaded with double-aught.

Best quote of the night:

Jay: Do you fish?

Luis: Nope. Oddly enough, I like to read about fishing. I like to read Tom McGuane write about fishing.

Jay: Hmph.

Luis: McGuane says trouts are smart. Wily. Are they?

Jay: Well, they're smarter than Tom McGuane.

Boulder, Rain, Friday.

A hippie woman has taken up temporary residence in the basement of our building. She has a squadron of stoned boys down there with her. All night last night she held court, the conversation rising through the floorboards with the pot smoke.

She began the conversation with her Ben-Wa balls: "I use the big ones," she was saying. "With the small ones, you really gotta work them." She then explained pornography, strippers, whores, and peep-shows to the adoring acolytes. "Guys jerk off in there," she said, giggling. "They have mirrors on the doors so they can see if the guy's in there jerking off!"

"Really?" one of the dudes replied.

They went through a catalog of dope-tinged subjects, including Dope. "It's a *healing* herb," one dude said. "It's a *gift!*"

Further interesting topics: cooking, the Grateful Dead, Jerry Garcia, The Rainbow People, trippin', LSD, mescaline, peyote, animals, bears, "fucked-up childhoods," parents, and how the Christians killed Magick.

Periodically, she would inform them that various people were "totally in awe of me."

By my count, there are at least seven people in the United States today living in a kind of religious rapture over her. The awe stemmed from whatever astonishing personal detail she was about to relate at the moment. Her sex life, her wanderings, her musings, her rock 'n' roll tastes, her dope consumption.

Her chipper egomania was oddly endearing and irritating at the same time. I was moved by how remarkable she took herself to be. And more, how sure she was that everybody else would find her amazing. Apparently, they did, since nobody told her to shut up. (And, after all, there I was in bed jotting down her musings.) Just like a writer!

When they got to hitchhiking—or "hikin'"—the stories got really rad, man. Full of perverts. Our hostess, of course, was *totally in control* on the road. But the boys had apparently been groped, fondled, and squeezed from Iowa to California. One dude was rescued from a "big homosexual trucker" by a "Dread." (Interestingly, nobody used any of the usual slang words for gay men. They always said "homosexuals.")

The "Dreadie" burst into the parked truck with a knife and "stabbed the dude in the fuckin' stomach." Then, all well in the Grateful Dead world, Deadhead and Dreadie walked off in the night, taking their small stand for harmony. Uh-huh, Dude, I thought.

I finally fell asleep around 3:00.

Rain, rain, don't go away. The weather is dark and mythical. Rain puts me in mind of my parents. I first think of my dad, but then I remember how my mom enjoyed thunder. My dad especially thrilled to driving in the rain. I have delicate and emotional memories of driving in rain with him. The rhythm of the windshield wipers, with their small mechanical whine and their tiny squeak at the end of their arc. The hum of the engine, the hiss of the tires. The oddly melancholy sound of passing cars, swishing like a linear wave cresting down a hundred-mile beach. The windows closed against the water; globes, gems, wiggling veins and amoebas of water collecting on the glass. Wind pushing drops up the edges of the windshield, where they'd gather and tremble at the top. The patter and drum of the water on the car. The radio on.

We seemed locked in a safe lozenge of space. It was a dim, shadowed vault of security. We were never closer, or safer-seeming, than in the car in rain. And we always watched eagerly for flooding. Nothing on earth was more pleasing on those days than wedges of water half-blocking intersections, tiny runoff rivers barreling down the gutters, churning little rapids in our streets that—immediately before the rain—were unexceptional. Were just tar and cement.

Did I ever tell you that—in '88—sitting in utter devastation in Indian Gardens, halfway down the Grand Canyon, I espied a small group of blond men speaking Spanish? The elder—the dad—wore a cowboy hat and Mexican boots, of all

things, and I said, "Excuse me, Sir, but are you Mexicans?"
Yes-yes, he said, and you? And I said, "Just my luck—I hike
down into the Grand Canyon and find another bunch of blond
Mexicans!" We all laughed and began the usual investigation—where are you from? They were from Sinaloa. I said
we were from Sinaloa. You're not an Urrea, are you? they
asked. Why, yes. The father said, "Are you the son of Beto
Urrea?" I . . . I . . . I am! I cried.

My God, the world is exactly four blocks long—there is
only one stop light, and it blinks all night.

Viva Las Vegas.

Stripped of its vestments of darkness and electric light, early-
morning Vegas is drab and pathetic. A scattering of supermarket architecture sheathed in smog.

Drive up and out, dreaming of Area 51: no UFOs in sight.

Flat deserts north of Vegas. Jet fighters chase each other
before jagged ridgelines. They look like Satan's arrowheads.
Ten-ton nuclear hornets. Vast lots of wrecked cars glitter in
the heat. They remind me of ranches, feedlots where old trucks
go to slaughter. Ford steaks. Prime ground Plymouth chuck.
Every sunbeam weighs exactly one pound.

Froggy-looking old bastard in a golf hat and a big American car, driving out. Heading into the wastelands. Carrying
an ever-heavier load of years and regrets and memories in the
trunk. Old eyes weak against the sun, hiding behind dark
glasses. He goes, lonesome. Heading Out There. To his des-
tiny. His dissolution. Just like me.

Cedar City, Utah.

Favorite sight: a small graveyard on a little rise, weedy head-stones and angled crosses. Directly behind it, an aluminum building with a big sign that says: TAXIDERMY.

Second favorite: a rusted-out black trailer from an abandoned big rig. On its side: HO HO HO.

Favorite town: Beaver.

Favorite road sign: EAGLES ON HIGHWAY.

I pause to sluice the Day-Glo guts of desert insects off the windshield.

Reading the stanzas of the day.

At the bottom of the grade, we decided to eat breakfast in a trucker's joint. I was interested in watching Mack pilots preparing themselves for the tedious and hot journey across the desert. I was singing James Brown: "I don't mind!" My friend said, "No, no, no. Don't talk like no black man in *here.*"

Perhaps he was right.

All around us were the red buttes and sunburned ravines of Big White Man. They were heaped around steaming mugs of coffee as though they'd been slapped in place by a hod carrier. Greatly in evidence were caps reading: REO. CAT. USA. WHITE.

Nobody turned around. There wasn't even any Red Sovine on the juke.

The bathroom was pristine: not a jot of graffiti. There were, however, machines selling three different types of prophylactic. On each machine, there was a lusty drawing of a wench in hot pants, all of them seen from behind and slightly below the knees. The psychology of this puzzled me for a moment. Why, for example, would a man about to embark on a journey across a few thousand barren, God-forsaken, evil miles need a "Tropical Colors" rubber? I was also curious about the pictures: one would assume that if a guy were going to drop fifty cents into one of these boxes, he'd pretty much already have his mind set on what it was for. Weren't they preaching to the converted? Maybe I had missed some important and mysterious aspect of manhood. Maybe things were just that way in the desert.

We were led to a booth beside a family of road graders. They were talking tractors—the big prehistoric Cats. The women were throwing around the same arcane mechanical jargon as the men. I was impressed.

My friend ordered chorizo and eggs.

The waitress said, "Is that huevos rancheros?"

"No," he said, "I'd like this one. The chorizo con huevos."

"Right. That one's huevos rancheros."

"No. I'd like this one, here, the, uh, chorizo and fried eggs. I *like* chorizo."

"Oh," she said. "I see."

I ordered an omelette. I got it, too. He got huevos rancheros.

Meanwhile, the head of the highway-scraper clan was telling this joke:

"So God calls Moses and says, Moses, I got good news, and I got bad news. And Moses says, Okay, God, gimme the good news.

"So God says, Moses, I'm gonna give you the power to part the Red Sea and escape the Egyptians.

"Moses goes, Hey, God, that's great! So what's the bad news?

"And God says, Well, the bad news is you've gotta make out an environmental impact report first!"

General hilarity overtook the table.

The house-sized boulders scattered on the hillsides were the powdery color of old women's faces.

We stopped in a cafe featuring "Home Style Cookin."

The old guy in the booth behind us started to choke on his food. His relatives flew into a panic. "Shut up," he snapped, staggering to the bathroom. He coughed and wheezed, a cranky old engine gone wild. The whole place paused, looking out of the corners of eyes, wondering if he'd come back out. His family sat, glued in place by his power.

He stormed out of the bathroom—it was hard to tell if anybody was relieved. Before his family could say anything, he said, "Just shut up. Shut the hell up."

"I ought to get your head examined," said his rumpled wife.

"Oh shut up," he said, as if life itself were the home fry caught in his throat.

Anza Borrego Desert.

We parked ourselves above Badlands Overlook. Some ocotillos were in bloom. The lava flows were so gone in years that they were reduced to vague dark splotches on the hardpan.

"Look, there's a big bug."

I looked—it was big, all right: a tarantula hawk was scooting around at the bottom of the slope. It looked nervous, like most wasps. Its nasty orange wings were popping the air above it. I casually tossed a rock at it to watch it take off. My aim was off that day: I hit it broadside.

The startled (I imagine) animal tumbled head-over-stinger in a shower of dirt. I can picture the bolt of surprise hitting its microchip brain. I felt guilty all day for that, blasting a creature who was only doing a day's work.

Unusual humidity on the coast had leaked over the mountains and knotted into grape-colored clouds. Vast wedges of flash-flood sands cut the desert into art deco patterns.

Shelter Valley had gotten an incredible ten inches of rain. The whole desert looked like a lawn. The gravel was green from the road to the hills. I had also stumbled into the butterfly blitz.

Waves and swarms covered the roads.

Black. Yellow. White.

Herds of skippers gathered on the blacktop in roughly circular groups. They wouldn't move for cars, and I found I could scoop my hand into the circle, and they'd climb all over it.

Crows ventured down from the hills and hopped from yucca stalk to yucca stalk, eyeing me and the butterflies, explaining it all to each other with a hearty, "croc!"

A couple of tons of cottontail were peeling out all over the place: brown fur bullets shot out of every arroyo and wash: lizards galore: hawks coasted the hot air rising off the road: stinkbugs stampeded through the masses of butterflies. Life was rampant in the house of heat and bones.

I took it personally.

"Lots of butterflies," the woman in the trading post said. "A while ago, it was millions of caterpillars. Caterpillars all over the place. They were everywhere you looked. Now we got butterflies."

My friend and I drove up past the Mormon Trail and left the truck. It was hot walking, and silent. We used beer for suntan lotion (an experiment with negligible results).

"I like ladies like that," he said.

"Me too."

I fed some beer to a creosote bush. Poured a little on a cholla.

"No bullshit."

"Who?"

"The lady."

"Yeah." I was touching all the plants.

"I'm in a no-bullshit mood."

"One thing's for sure, those ladies are straight-shooters."

In my mind, I was suddenly in cowboy boots. Italian cowboys were about to descend from the red crags. I stopped and listened for the Ennio Moriconne theme music. Looked for the close-up on Eastwood.

I was in Canyon Without A Name (Cañon Sin Nombre).

The desert proceeded to play its weird tricks: I heard women laughing.

There was no one there. The closest people were in a Cessna cruising far above the ridgeline.

I was standing there, watching the plants grow, when the women giggled.

I looked around—lots and lots of nothing. Lizard tracks. Dead things. What could have been deer or sheep or goat tracks. The funny etchings lizards leave in the dust.

But no women. Only their unearthly voices.

There would come a bit of a word, as though shattered and still whirling in the air. A half echo. A gasp.

Were they ghosts? Was it the wind?

Voices from across the desert, bounced at me by some thermal space warp?

Perhaps I was hearing voices from the past, voices that had been eddying in the canyons for hundreds of years. Maybe I was hearing the age-old laughter of Indian girls; maybe I heard the sound of Mormon women who had wandered off the Mormon Trail to do laundry or bathe at the small oasis, having a laugh about their common husband.

Sirens.

Nymphs.

Dryads.

Birds.

Crickets.

Demons.

An alternative universe folding itself into this one for an instant.

Or maybe I was hearing my own ancestors stirring, waking up in my bones, climbing up my genes and diving, bare and glistening, into my blood.

Out we went, leaving the truck stop in the west. The desert, instead of turning starker and more sere, went green. I was dismayed, confused. It was like a hallucination: cotton, tomatoes, cultivation. Some maniac had been irrigating the desert.

"What kind of a desert is this!" I wanted to know.

We turned down a side road, under a churning column of smoke, imagining conflagration, apocalypse, the destruction of Sodom.

It was a guy burning off his field.

We were deflated.

We were lost.

In the middle of this nightmare of desert farmland, we found Mexican stoop-laborers hoeing and picking, yanking up some vegetable under the watchful gaze of a white boss. It was like stumbling upon a hidden sin, some secret atrocity.

"Look at that," I said.

"Wish I had a camera," he said.

They were using short hoes. I could almost hear their spines creak, the blood steaming inside their flesh in the heat.

"I bet the foreman would love that," I said.

There was an old Ford bus in the field, and a portable john tilted on its wheels. Tiny white ibis picked their way along the rows, spearing bugs with their elegant beaks.

People tearing their own bodies apart so we can eat salads. Every mouthful soaked in sweat.

High, metal clouds.

The light seemed subaqueous. It was like hiking across the ocean floor. I was in a cattle-skull frenzy, but there were no skulls to be found.

Evidence of the recent flooding and the lone track of a motorcycle scarring the land. A silence so wide and clear and pure; an absence of sound; a weight of stillness that nestles in the ear and feels good. I could hear people talking in a silver trailer across the road, about a quarter mile distant. A B-52 rode its column of snowy steam.

Things I discovered: a set of mouse tracks in the soft sand along a dry bank in a wash; these were met by a set of bird tracks; then a scuffle; finally, no tracks at all. The most vital story in the world, written in dust.

Slow ants. An odd piece of rusted metal, wadded like cloth and jammed deep in the crust. Fast ants. A can shot full of holes. New burrows with rings of fresh sand around their irregular mouths. A piece of wood, under which were three residents: one small spider with stubby legs, one large beetle who was mottled to look like a rock and playing dead, one lizard smaller than my little finger wearing many colors. They all obviously wished I'd go home and watch TV.

A silvery cylinder with fins like a small rocket. A bunch of empty leathery eggs, looking like long-rotted oranges.

Later, I found a little rattler. It was curled up under a lip of stone, still drowsy in the cool air. It looked solid and dense as a wood carving. I wanted to wake it up, but my friend protested.

We chose, instead, to hike up a wash and see what was between two southern crags. As we waded through the white sand, we inspected the buffalo gourds, stinky things that love to grow in open spaces. I had given up on cow skulls and was searching the edges of the wash, hoping erosion had knocked loose a few fossils. I found a black stone covered with feathery white traces. I dropped it in my pocket. I was going to make a joke, when a car sped out of the opening in the hills, ahead. We stopped and watched it come at us.

"Maybe we ought to get out of here," my friend said.

We started to back up, but the car went by us, throwing up a tall plume of dust. We watched it hit the highway, hang a sharp left, toward civilization, and take off.

We stood there, laughing at this peculiar event. We started to walk up the wash again, when we heard the sound. I think I heard it first. In fact, I think I felt it first—it was more an unease in my ear than an actual sound.

"Hear that?" I said.

"Yeah," he said.

It was a throb, a pulse. It became a *whop-whop*. He turned around. "It's a helicopter!"

The machine blasted out of the wash, swung toward us, and flew like a tarantula hawk. Suddenly, we were in a *Fortean Times* strange event. A UFO fiend/militia man's nightmare: the helicopter was completely black. A flat black, with no high-lights at all. Its nose was dipped a little, as though the machine was staring at us. We froze. There were no insignia anywhere on it, no lettering, not even a registration number. Until that moment, I had believed the black helicopters were an urban myth. But there it was, bearing down on me, and it was big.

The side door was open, and there was a man visible with dark goggles over his eyes and a helmet hiding the rest of his head. He was staring at us. The helicopter's harsh black shadow slapped us and was by in an instant.

The unmarked beast went straight down the wash, crossed the road, and kept going, deep into the heart of the desert. Heading north.

We were terrified and delighted.

Had the speeding car discovered something dastardly? Were they drug smugglers being chased by the DEA? Escapees from some Steve King scenario? Or illegal aliens making a run for the kitchen of the McDonald's in El Cajon?

And the helicopter?

"Uh," my bud said, "I think it's time to go home now."

I raced him to the truck.

Desert.

Far from dead.

The notion of bigness is small beside it.

The sky is so high that I once saw a rainbow form a full circle.

God's footprint. Ground zero.

The skeletal feeling of bare rock, spiny riblike plants, silver cactus hulks. Inside these dead cacti, owls the size of hamsters.

So much room that the smallest detail looms, vast and full of meaning: the tiniest purple flower, when seen against the distance, completely covers a mountain.

At night, you bruise your head against the stars.

And the stones, they seem alive to me. They're lying out there tonight, cold and sparkling. If you see them in the right light—a full moon, stripped ivory by the wind, or the pre-dawn light, the color of old nickels—those stones seem to form bodies, faces.

They look like the earth is sleeping, dreaming. Waiting for that miraculous call to rise. To rise in the heat and dance.

Boulder.

Reading A. R. Ammons, *Sumerian Vistas.*

I have often joked that Mr. Ammons' greatest gift to me as a writer was the colon. But it's not that much of a joke, really. The man's poems are colon-crazy. He wants to make us *see* so much that he grabs our collars, rubs our faces in the words. And those colons lodge in you, they nudge you as you look at a blackbird, or a 1949 pickup truck with hay in the bed and a dog with a bandanna sitting in the driver's seat. The Ammons punctuation punctuates the world, not just the page. He says: look: *look:* LOOK: *LOOK.*

For a while there, I was writing poems logjammed with colons because of him: poems that didn't move like they should: but which stopped: every few feet: to try to see: every:thing: it was all: deserving: of: study:!

The first section of *Sumerian Vistas* is one of his long *Ina Gadda Da Vida* + drum solo poems, "The Ridge Farm." There is a small incident in this poem that haunts me, makes me look for gopher tunnels as I stroll, makes me stop and think about small bones beside the trail. It was so sad, it stunned me for a minute. I actually stopped reading, put the book down and thought about it, picked it back up and re-read it, then I read it to someone else.

In short, a mole falls into a watering can. Ammons writes of finding it later, when he goes out to water a pot of strawberry plants. He had thought the plants dead, but they had revived on their own (death and life, as always, crossing and intersecting in life and art). He at first mistakes the mole, drowned, for a rat, and he's pithy and witty and offhand about the stinking corpse, until an unexpected flash of compassion and vision breaks the heart:

> the rat was a mole: the arctic air
> yesterday afternoon dried him out and
> the freeze last night stiffened him much
> reduced in size and scent: so
> I broke out the shovel, dug up a
> spade, dumped in the mole: there let
> him rot, the rat: I can see how
> something blind could get into my
> wateringcan: but those feet!
> I can hear him scratching up the side:
> to get in, or out: but also I can hear him
> sloshing, the blind water darkened by
> night, till nobody came.

Good God! What a small and immense tragedy. All the sorrow and hardness of Nature comes rushing in at me when I read that. I think of the picturesque deer gracing my lawn, all hung with ticks like bloody Christmas ornaments. It's terrible and it's wonderful out there, as it is in the pages of any great book.

Ammons tells us: everything is safe for poems.

And: everything is dangerous.

Oct. 12. Columbus Day/Culon's Day.

We marched on the Regents' Office at CU. It was amazing, walking along with the Umas and Oyate and black students and all the rest. Rick Williams in his Sioux braids. A vibrant moment of unity as the "minorities" took a 1960s action to serve notice that the university would have to get serious about its claims and promises of diversity. "Minority?" one speaker said. "I'm not minor."

Then, last night, we drove with Janet Hard and Mark Saunders into the Rockies in the Jeep. We took sleeping bags and coats and gloves and hats and coffee and binoculars. We drove into wonderfully eerie nighttime Rocky Mountain National Park, and down into the Fall River valley. We settled in on a bend in the road and listened to the elks bugle. Excited steam-blowing Coloradans stood in murmuring groups, thrilled to freeze and listen to horny herd animals squeal. Earlier, I had joined the traffic jams of other—perhaps these same—Coloradans going high to see the aspens change color. *This,* I thought, *is the place for me.* A place where everything depends on the color of a leaf, on the voice of an elk.

Their cries echoed all over the hills, and their battles

rattled: antlers enmeshed and clattering like wooden chairs clacking together.

Above, the Milky Way—Diana's Milk, the Spine of the Heavens—ran at an angle due west. Shooting stars. Satellites moved steadily, amber as they reflected the sun. A jetliner flew over us, unaware that four humans were upthrust on a jag of rock and closer to their belly than they could have dreamed. "Someone up there," I said, "is watching a Goldie Hawn movie."

Prairie fire!

Bright, hot, golden, vast, pure. Mysteriously beautiful. Always moving. Sends up biblical columns of smoke by day. A purifier of the prairies. The grasses require it to clean the earth; old stems, weeds, bushes, dead stalks are burned away. The charcoal fertilizes the soil. Locusts burn and pop. Native animals flee. The grass knows that when the fire passes, seeds must drop. Cleared ground allows sun to ignite germination. All is renewed and brought to life by the fearsome hot death that swept through. If the Creator didn't start the flame with lightning, the tribes themselves lit the torch. Everything must burn so that everything may grow.

There is something of us in this.

Deep purple frowns of rain pull the sky into the shortgrass. We're in Blessed Colorado, the mad peaks jutting hard into the floor of Heaven. Oh man—the spires of impossible millennia break open the sky. The stratosphere is shattering. Huge pieces crash to the ground all around us: a flash-flood in a canyon fifty miles away; a wall of rain as far across as a San Diego suburb; a hill full of sun and six valleys brimming with shadow. The land is silver, tawny, gold, green, red, dusky blue, yellow. Horses. Orange tractors and rubber road cones. Radio towers. The angry cloud bellies looking like a storm-whipped sea inverted by a cosmic Dali or Magritte, tacked upside down above us with golden pins. Upside-down whales, sharks, dolphins above the oceanclouds. The galaxies are starfish. The moon is a shell. The rain is the spray of the inverted slow motion grape juice storm surf celestial sea.

God is a surrealist.

I went out to harvest fallen aspen leaves to mail to friends today. I drove all up in the mountains, then wandered down along a dirt road that wound behind rocky peaks—three, four, *six* eagles circled their nests atop the peak! Wide as the Jeep. Slow. Turning like the hands of some huge sacred clock, or the pages of a celestial calendar we can't fathom. Silent as fog.

I sat by a lake and was immediately surrounded by curious marmots. Marmot detectives splayed on top of the boulders and peered down at me, squinting. They hustled from bush to bush, like GIs in a black-and-white movie attacking a machine-gun nest. Secret whistles between the troops. All they needed were trench coats, sunglasses, steel helmets, tommy guns.

A woodpecker, bright white with black boxes all over his

feathers, jumped on a tall weed and swung back and forth on it like it was a carnival ride. Whee!

I found a slender baby snake with a black head. He tried to act like a rattlesnake to scare me, but it was like being attacked by a wet shoelace. I had to respect his spirit. He swirled away, certain of his ferocity, his mastery of all the shore.

Fishermen in the distance tried to fool wily fish into committing suicide.

The leaves on the gravel and in the mud. Golden coins. Small yellow hearts fallen away before the cold.

Stood outside in the post-midnight dark to look at the stars. Cold Rocky air licking my skin. Cool beneath my clothes as refreshing as a drink of water. Bits and pieces of my soul scattered and burning among the stars. Crickets still call, singing against winter. And five miles away, the echoing voice of a dog. I want to cut myself down the middle, pull my body open, let all the burning and the stink and the blood fly out. I want to fill with cold mountain air. I'm burning up. I want to rain on the window of a lonely reader.

I want to launch, throwing sparks, up through the night.

winter

Year-end revelling . . .
still in pilgrim's cape must I
roam my endless road.
—*Basho*

This is the time of year when the roadside streams are turning milky and opaque, slowing down in their endless rush and starting to yawn. Grass is brittle as glass underfoot, crackling as you walk. Freezing rain covers all bare branches and makes them look like they were blown in a glass factory in Europe, delicate tinkling ornaments of ice. The crows are just sick about it. Cottonwoods stand bare against the solid blue air, etching Japanese letters against the small snow. The haiku of coldness.

The whole world is frozen and friendly.

"You would have to care about the land," Tom McGuane wrote at the beginning of *Nobody's Angel*. Whenever it gets cold, and snowy days are upon us, I want to pull that book off the shelf and read it again. Ol' Tom seems to fall in and out of favor, and since the great Montana writer's cliche has set in to American letters they may not want to take him to heart in the big world—who knows. But for me, *Nobody's Angel* is a perfect book. It may be one of the saddest books, but it is also one of the funniest, and its pages are full of a spring light that is hard to explain. Snow days are good days for a touch of spring to glow out of a book.

If nothing else, it features one of my favorite tumbling mad sentences. And if anyone can write a mad sentence, it's Tom McGuane. He writes: "The yard light erect upon its wood stanchion threw down a yellow faltering glow infinitely chromatic falling through the China willow to the ground pounded up against the house by the unrepentantly useless horses." Go, Tom! Later in the book there is the startling epiphany of a man realizing that the middle of his brain might just look like an asshole.

I bought *Nobody's Angel* in the heart of a different winter, in the big bookstore on Hollywood Boulevard. I was staying with Shawn Phillips up in his charmed house in the hills above the city. It was a house of wind chimes and toys: aside from Shawn's mammoth synthesizer setup and myriad guitars, there was a Van der Graff generator in the corner, looking like a prop from a Frankenstein movie. Clutching the electric coil at the top lurked an Alien replica. I'd been sleeping on the floor with one of the roadies for the Moody Blues.

I had gone from being a Shawn Phillips fan to a friend, beginning with a small book of poems delivered to the stage at a concert in San Diego years before. Shawn was on tour with the Moody Blues, and this very roadie had accepted my small book and carried it backstage. Now here he was, snoring beside me on the floor and during the day trying to cure my cold with cayenne pepper capsules and beer.

And Shawn, now that we were friends, put me in touch with his amazing father, the espionage writer, Philip Atlee. And Atlee—Jim was his real name—was one of the first writers to take me under his wing, give me spy/poet feedback on my work. And both Shawn and Jim gave me the immense blessing of offering me the daily Christmas gift of stepping down from the idol's pedestal and allowing me to feel like a peer.

Perhaps the greatest training was watching Shawn "do fame." He did fame really well, treating every strange fan as if he or she were the most important fan in the world. People who no one else would even look at, Shawn stared at as if they were angels. Even the madwoman who, after John Lennon was shot, appeared backstage with a mango that had obviously been punctured repeatedly with a needle, injected with who knows what weird recipe. He graciously accepted the mango, shook her hand, and told her he'd be coming out that door over there—exactly opposite from where he'd be coming out—in about half an hour. She drifted out and we locked the door behind her. We all stared at the killer mango, then it went in the trash.

Or one day when we were walking up Selma toward Hollywood. I was already in a daze because I saw some of the Wall of Voodoo boys staggering down the street. Shawn couldn't have cared less about Wall of Voodoo: he wanted a hot dog.

We stopped at a Korean hot dog stand, and as we sat there in weenie smoke, a maniac rushed up to us on our stools and said, "What are they, Chinese?"

He slyly, he believed, shot glances at the cooks, tipped his head at them.

Shawn filled his gob with hot dog and gazed benignly at him. I just shrugged.

"You Vietnamese?" the guy shouted. "Or what?"

"Korean," the woman said.

The maniac perked up.

"Korean! We sure showed those fuckin communists something in Korea, huh?"

He turned to us. Shawn filled his mouth with Pepsi and looked blank. Coward. I was catching on to him.

The maniac leaned in to me.

"Didn't we kick some God-damned Chinese commie ass in Korea? Well we sure as hell did!"

The maniac asked me if he could borrow my pen.

I handed it to him.

FUCKIN' COMMUNISTS! he wrote.

And, later, after I had taken comfort for a few years in *Nobody's Angel,* and Shawn and I had both been through sorrows, Jim Phillips died too soon, loves faded, careers gave us endless grief, I got up the gumption to send McGuane a fan letter. I told him how his book had seen me through some difficult winters. And McGuane wrote back. No stranger to difficult winters himself, he said: "Even Richard Nixon said life is basically ninety-nine rounds."

Nobody can cuss like Duane Brewer, at Pine Ridge, South Dakota. Nobody can snore like Duane, either, but when he cusses, he sings hymns, he composes epics.

Over the phone, he tells me that one of his enemies is:

"A low-life, mother-effin', shit-lipped, et up, dried out, box of Kentucky Fried Chicken."

Amen.

I must be part marmot: winter comes and I burrow in, barely write, eat chili and stare at televangelists, wondering when the next snowstorm is coming, amazed when it comes that the earth at 3:00 A.M., after the clouds have rolled out to the plains, glows beneath the moon like the grand night light that it is: every sound caught in the white and hugged to silence.

Winter: work-time. Heater pumping. Depeche Mode, the Nephilim, C. C. Adcock, John Campbell, Yello, the Groundhogs, Jimi, Kate Bush, R. L. Burnside booming on the stereo. Three-legged foxhound resting against my feet. Snow dropping in loose spirals like confetti. I scribble away at a novel, much of it a love song to these Rockies, trying to capture the feel of the land:

> Tom couldn't stop shaking.
>
> He drove the pickup along the fold where the high plains rose into the Front Range. The swollen moon set the landscape to glowing: the grasses were a silvery mist all around them. Far off to their left, planes stacking up over the Denver airport looked like spaceships hovering over the sea.
>
> The mountains in front of them and to their right were a blackness against the dark. It looked to Tom as though the bottom edge of night had shattered, and the ragged negative space filling the horizon might be another world, deeper and older, hidden on the other side of the sky. It was almost as if he could swing the wheel west, and instead of smashing into the hills, he could drive through, into space, into heaven or hell or someplace utterly more wonderful and strange. Just drive into the ether. Speed into a night without stars.
>
> Bobo sat silent beside him.
>
> The lights of Longmont, Louisville, Lafayette. Far Denver. And, after an extended silence, Boulder,

tucked into the valley at the foot of the Flatirons. It looked like a thousand fireflies had landed in a field right before them. It didn't look like houses five miles away. Boulder—you could scoop it up in one hand and blow on it, watch the lights flicker and flutter. Glow.

Bobo nudged him.

"There's Whoville," he said.

"Yes," Tom replied, trying out the word, seeing if he could speak at all.

Bobo said, "You know Boulder? They get their drinking water off a glacier. You ever seen a glacier?"

Tom shook his head.

"Me neither. Arapaho Glacier."

He drummed his cane on the floor of the truck. One, two. Three. Four.

"We ain't never seen a glacier, Gringo," he said. "But we can drink a little piece of one whenever we feel like it. Isn't that something?"

And it was. Tom nodded, smiled, drunk and sleepy. It was something. It really was. Something too wonderful to even understand.

This road.

This life.

I have an amusing stone and a deer legbone that the mountains gave me back in the fall. As I got to know the trails better, the lions and the peaks left gifts for me at certain prearranged spots. At one hidden beach along the tumbling creek, I found this round stone, etched with a natural bull's eye, sitting exactly in the center of a round boulder also colored in rings. It looked like a snowman with racing stripes. And beside it, the bone. I keep them by my computer. They remind me to be thankful.

At that spot, I collected the gifts and stared at the water. It was rushing by and spreading out, shallow and cold, the sleep of winter coming on. I was thinking about Richard Brautigan's *Trout Fishing in America,* and the scene where the narrator goes into a hardware store that is selling trout streams by the foot. He wanders into their lumber yard and finds stacked lengths of stream. I think he buys about three yards or so and carries them out to his car.

I realized I had to do something similar with this creek. Just cut a piece out and study it. So I pulled off shoes and socks like the kid I imagine I once was but most probably never got the chance to be. And I built a dam! A middle-aged idiot stacking river stones in the creek.

The silt settled back down after I stopped splashing around. The mottled bottom revealed itself—grit and rocks, fool's gold, maybe real gold (I like to think so), the endless dapple of underwater sun. I stood there, my feet frozen, white as fish bellies. I do believe I could have cut that section out with a knife and carried it away, thrown over my shoulder like those Mexican burlap sacks of beans.

Cross-country snow-drive. Haunted Rocky valleys made over into ice chasms. Lonesome high-country rest area well beyond Frisco. Colorado of the great place-names: Hygiene, Rifle, Parachute, Fountain, Silt, Gunbarrel. I'm surprised we don't have a town called Ham Sandwich, or Hemorrhoid.

Snowflakes the size of dandruff. I'm wearing a Kerouac T-shirt, a black vest, a Colorado Division of Wildlife cap. The wet ribbon of 1-70 smokes below me in the winter sun. A chipper bird sits on the fence rail before me, flicking its tail jauntily and considering this white weather.

A snowplow driver has survived one of our many avalanches by burying his rig inside a small tunnel. He sat and smoked with the engine running until somebody came with a tractor and scooped him out. I wonder if he was reading a book. I wonder if he was listening to Johnny Cash. Oh bury me any day beside Johnny Cash.

All the road has been alive with incident and visions. The buffalo family south of Boulder stood with icy beards and breathed fire. Each mountain of the Front Range had a dense belt of fogcloud cinched tight to its belly, holding up its trousers of ponderosas and lodgepoles. Waterfalls burst out of ice walls, some of them as frozen in the air as melted candle wax.

Streams were still powerful, biting off hunks of shore ice: wide backs full of rippling muscles, logs held in their teeth. Dead elk lying like small horses beside the road. I remember one morning finding run-down elk scattered along the Buffalo Bill's Grave turnoff, and all their heads had been chainsawed off and carted away. The deep shock of red from each neck stump, making of the corpses something else entirely, something alien and frightening.

A semi jackknifed on the downgrade of i-70. One brave cop at 5:30 A.M. parked halfway up the mountain, cutting off the lanes, lights flashing a warning. Crushed yellow fenders, gone in a flash, and rock slides gone just as fast. At Georgetown, white mountain goats lined the freeway, feeding on brittle weeds and oblivious to the wrecks or the avalanches. They were always in pairs, and each pair was paired with a second pair, and each set of pairs was spaced about a half mile apart.

Now, in a small valley below me, what looks like a marmot waddles through the snow. I watch him with my binoculars.

Mad Kerouac on the tape deck, muttering Bop Haikus:
The little worm
lowers itself from the roof
on a self-shat thread.

Onward!
Fifty miles later, a crow so lazy it walks out of the fast lane, cars brushing its tail.

All the peaks wear cowboy hats of cloud.

Air so crisp and clean you feel you could crunch it in your mouth.

Horses dreaming in the rain.

To hell with dreaming! Donkey trots across the flooded cold field. Cursing.

Utah at 11:52 A.M.

Behind me, the road was so wet that each car traveled in its own silver cloud of spray. All down the road, small storm fronts sped along between the lines. Semis were miniature hurricanes.

Ahead, Utah is a panorama of shades of red. Clouds above look like yellow and blue Maxfield Parrish extravaganzas. I'm driving into a 1938 barbershop calendar.

Listening to Cactus Ed Abbey, now, reading on the deck. Jack tried too self-consciously to be poetic. Ed tried too self-consciously to be non-poetic. Both poor drunk dead bastards ended up creating poetry in spite of themselves.

I stand behind the WELCOME TO UTAH sign, with its painted landscape, and squint so it covers part of the real landscape. I'm making my own mental Magritte paintings on the side of the road while Ed intones a litany of insults to cows, and truckers slow, spray me with road drizzle, and wonder what no-good strangeness I'm up to.

I don't know, Jack and Ed—maybe poetry made *you*. Maybe the vast beyond chose you and wrote on you. I tip my cap to both of them, and I drive on, wishing I could call them on the phone and say, "Now what?"

Road hallucination: I just saw what I'd swear was a chopped off white man's hand laying in the fast lane.

Pulled off to visit a roadside Utah outhouse. Coyote tracks circle the small stone building. Coyotes circling the heady stench in the snowy darkness.

I could smell the outhouse myself from twenty feet away.

I walked in and was appalled to find that some traveler had voided his bowels all over the room. Colonic graffiti was everywhere—the poor man must have gone off like fireworks.

I walked over to the edge of the canyon and sat on the rocks. Wanted to clear my nose with the scent of sage and ice. A white rabbit slunk away from me. People coming out of the toilet cast suspicious glances at me. I can read their thoughts: *That's the low-down son of a bitch who set off the poo-bomb in the outhouse!* The edges of the canyon are set out in steps and porches. Thunder goes off like dynamite blowing holes in the clouds. Some spray-can philosopher has written ETERNAL DISNEYLAND for us to ponder. Deep down the canyon, a tire. At my feet, a tampon applicator.

Somewhere out there, Green River holds up hunks of ice, turns them slowly, and ponders all their facets.

I watched a fire truck tear up Flagstaff Mountain in the dark. Its lights flashed small and bright. Its desperate voice echoed over Boulder. It strained back and forth up those 10-mph switchbacks. Utter blackness. The only thing moving on the land. It seemed the most lonesome speck of light on earth.

I was walking home today . . . alone . . . lonely . . . abandoned . . . freezing . . . frostbitten . . . when this guy hurried past wearing ill-fitting running shoes that went: GWEEP! GWEEP! GWEEP! And I thought, Ain't life great?

A Definition of "Friend."

You won't get dependent on me. I'm just a letter. I'm a dream. You have a life of your own, just as I do. You have the massive Work of your Days, the Creation of your Days to attend to. You have your own needs and hungers and those of your family. I'm here when you need the dream time. I'm here for you when you're sweating poems, when the bathroom door's closed and your heart's seeking as you lie back in the water. I'm off to the side—see me?—in the woods. Tonight, the earth is cold, and I light myself for you so you will be warm. I'll give you what light I can spare so you can see to read those poems, what heat is in me so your hands won't shake. And later, when the sun returns, on hot days when nobody can see you, you can run over here under the blue spruce and the Douglas fir and the lodgepole pines and the quaking aspen and the cotton-woods and the bristlecones (all sacred) and grab the cool dipper and drop it in the well and take a drink. You can sip, you can gulp. I stay open all day. And at night, when the fingernail moon is a thin crescent, and the bats hurry on their paths, you come out in your long white gown and grab a drink. That's what I'm for. And I expect the same from you. Whether I've been good or bad, whether I've worked hard or indolently gazed at the peaks all day, no matter how I voted or how long the dishes have sat dirty in my sink. When I need to drink, you will wet my lips. That is my definition of Friend.

For some reason, I bought a hand grenade today. I keep it by the computer. It strikes me as funny, but I can't explain why. It must be a BOY THING. Bugs and bombs. I cain't hep myseff.

One of our wonderful I-can-wear-shorts-in-midwinter days today. I went to the Mesa Trailhead, outside Eldorado Springs, aiming for Devil's Thumb: grind the aerobics and feel my spit turn to glue. As I walked, a small group of men with Down Syndrome came out of the brush. They were being led by a hearty Outward Bound type. "Excuse us," the guide said. The men clutched each other's hands and shirttails. I stepped aside.

The walkers were *transported*. Their faces were all lit up like motel signs. The sun, the mountains, the bugs, the trees: they could not contain their joy. Some of them couldn't speak, but they still could not stay quiet. "Hi!" I said.

They stopped. They put their hands in the air, pointing. One of them yelled. A pure cry of praise.

"Yes," I said.

Huge smiles. Bobbing heads. Loud voices. We laughed and patted each other. All around us, the last sturdy insects rattled in the dead weeds. All of the men in their group opened their palms to the sun and closed their eyes. Utterly there. They taught me, on that dirt, how to walk.

There I was, walking a poem.

Shirttail Peak. Devil's Thumb. Shadow Canyon. Homestead, Towhee, Mesa, Big Bluestem Trails.

Coming back down, I heard a small sound that seemed to

rasp against the sizzling of grounded leaves in the breeze. Dry rhythm. Faint, determined. A rustle. I was with my three-legged foxhound who, although running on less than four-wheel drive, still pulled me straight up over enthusiastic elevations. He didn't find this small rasp of any interest, and wandered off to see how many cactus pads he could embed in his face.

I got on my hands and knees and crawled around like an aardvark, following that sound. You could tell the sound had a purpose—though perhaps the purpose was to make me look like a stooge. Dog and man, seen from a distance, looked like they were each sniffing fabulous puddles of coyote pee and about to lift a leg.

The tiny sound pulled me down to a triangular wedge of piled grass and leaves between two boulders. The grasses bunched, lifted, moved forward. I crawled back. The wad of detritus fell. I moved forward. Here it came again! I shuffled back. My dog lifted his head, looked at me, shook his head sadly, then buried his face in a crumbling cowflop.

I was thrilled! I thought: *a mouse*. I thought: *a pack rat*. I thought: *a rattlesnake*. Suddenly, it burst out. A beetle!

A beetle the size of a mouse!

Its great shiny black head broke through, and its mandibles opened in my face. They looked like elk antlers.

How do you do? it said.

I'm quite well, thank you, I replied. *And you?*

Oh! Well, Dear Boy—what with winter and all, a fellow simply can't afford a coffee break!

Quite right, my Good Man!

Toodle-oo, Old Sport, it said. *See you in the spring! Oh, and by the way—should you decide to try to pick me up, I shall indubitably bite the living hell out of you.*

He did a U-turn and drove back into the humus like a tractor. Just arranging the furniture. Just getting squared away. Decorating the comfy bug condo for Christmas.

On the way down the mountain, the dog was astonished to discover a horse, a palomino in the middle of the trail, glowing in the icy sun. The lone cowboy on its back—black hat, red plaid coat, tan gloves—made elaborate efforts to keep from looking at me. He, like the beetle, was hoping I'd just go away. But the dawg wouldn't move. He and the horse stood there, staring at each other. Animal ESP.

What in the hell are you? the dog said.

I know what you are, the horse replied, *but what are you doing way up here?*

I've got to lead this dumb human around so he doesn't get lost. I'm trying to get him down to the creek so we can get a drink, the dog said.

Tell me about it, Bub, said the horse. *I've gotta carry this lazy son of a bitch up the mountain on my back!*

"Come on, boy," I said. The dog followed me down the trail, all the time looking over his shoulder. *Man,* he was saying, *that was the biggest dog I ever saw!* On the way to the creek he peed on twenty-eight bushes and stones and wagged his tail like crazy.

Went to the lake with the tripod hound for a quick walk be-fore the snow. Or, I should say, a quick *pull*. If it would only snow, I could ski behind him.

Sadness of snow clouds.

A stillness lay over the land, spread across the houses out here on the edge of town. Late afternoon: porch lights on the hill, orange bug-lights, could be seen as campfires one hun-dred years ago. The highest tips of the Flatirons being erased by the first invasion of mists.

Canada geese, seemingly reluctant to continue their jour-neys, have congregated on the lake. They are divided into two distinct groups, and they hang out on either side of the penin-sula that carries the walking path over a small bridge. They forage and feed on the lawns. They don't mingle, and they don't seem to pay attention to each other. When a jogger, or a dog, or a roving Boulder pothead in an oversize army coat comes along, each flock turns its back on the other and begins to stroll into the water. They don't hurry, just pull in a well-woven mass across the grass, occasionally honking in irrita-tion. They spread like a blanket onto the water and ice.

The half-formed ice sheet pinged and hummed as it moved.

There was one curious touch: in the north flock, a single white goose. As the flocks parted to let us pass, this one white goose at the farthest edge of the big gray gang of Canadians hustled along behind them, head down, making more noise than they. It jumped in the patch of clear water and swam behind them, seeming . . . lonesome, somehow.

The tripod and I went off around the lake, and he found ways to urinate every few steps while balancing on two legs.

Often, he'd rest the raised leg against the tree or pole he was anointing, thus anchoring himself firmly. I enjoyed watching his nose read the olfactory *New York Times* spread out across the land: goose droppings—"Aha! Yes, yes, fascinating." A poodle's puddle—"You don't say!" A fragrant paw print and a raccoon's nest in a drainpipe—"Well, well! Did you ever!"

Rounding the far end of the lake, we stumbled on a hidden focal point that redefined the scene. We were following the shore, inspecting stones and muddy prints, when a little red bedspread caught my eye. I thought it had been discarded after being torn, and the white cotton stuffing was pouring out. We wandered over for a sniff—to the dog this was like turning to the "Lifestyles" section of the paper. He was giving the quilt a close inspection when I realized a shiny black eye was staring up from the wad of white cotton.

I pulled back the bedspread, and there was a dead white goose, lying on its side. Its beak was open, its bright orange feet almost crossed, its wings tangled, feathers intertwined like fingers.

I looked out at the big Canadians floating in the water, and at the lone white goose skirting their perimeter. I realized suddenly that the scene I had anthropomorphized as being lonely, *was* lonely. It was fully and honestly sad. And as the dog and I stood over these empty remains that some fellow wanderer had tucked in against the impossible cold, I was convinced that the one white bird amidst so much gray was watching us, was honking and crying directly at us.

I could not imagine the journey ahead.

Santa Fe. December 13.

The marquee said: JOE ELY TEXAS ROCK LEGEND.

All sorts of fascinating Santa Fe humanoids were coming in the door, and I was enjoying the sightings: lots of big fat 48-year-old men with long hair; rock and roll women who don't mind being called babes; a smattering of bikers; New Age faux cowboys; three real cowboys; a barrel-chested man with extremely short arms and legs with Hells Angel whiskers, a scowl, a leather vest, and a cane; waitresses with trays and high round perky cocktail waitress bottoms; a man with the neck of a stud bull in a T-shirt that said GOD DON'T MAKE NO JUNK. (Somebody else I'd heard about had been seen in a shirt with the motto: I AM BAD CRAZY.)

Among these crowds came a blind man, or a mostly blind man—he squinted in the gloom and tipped his head and his eyes rolled back and forth and he seemed to see the lights on the wall, for he focused on them with a kind of wonder on his face. He had a white cane that was almost as tall as he was. He held it up under his chin and poked at the floor as he maneuvered near our table. He turned his face up to the lamp above my head and said, "Oh boy!"

This man had the sweetest face in the world. Everything about him, in fact, radiated sweetness. I know that we romanticize the blind, and shame on us. We create scenarios where they're kind and long-suffering, sensitive and saintly. But this man, blind or not, was sweet. He wore a T-shirt with a drawing of a cat on it that could only be called a kitty. Over it, an unbuttoned untucked work shirt. White jeans that he'd only zipped up halfway. He smiled at the light, put his hand over his brow as if there were a burning sun above him, and squinted his eyes almost closed as he tried to force just a little more focus into them so he could see more light. Presently, a friend came for him and led him away, toward the stage.

What happened was, two young Indian men came in and cased the joint. One of them was just a beer-lovin' Ozzie Osbourne fan in a flannel shirt and a soft belly, hopeful whiskers. The other guy was a warrior, no way around it. He was handsome and fierce, and he knew it. Possessed of a perfect narrow-waisted body and wide shoulders, in skin-tight new jeans and a skin-tight dark blue shirt. He had volumes of shiny black hair that hung all the way down to his belt. He looked like Wind-In-His-Hair in *Dances with Wolves*. He wore a pager hooked on his belt—at first, I mistook it for a knife. He nursed a beer, and maintained a vaguely amused look on his face, and basically appeared to be ready to trounce everybody in the bar. He had a high round perky perfect cocktail waitress bottom.

White boys, even the bikers, steered clear of him. They hurried nervously when they got to him, as if he were planning a personal Battle of the Little Bighorn. And he'd see them, chuckle, nudge his bud, and gesture at the scuttling gringos with his beer bottle.

In that room, Custer had definitely died for our sins.

Then Joe Ely came on and *rocked*.

Suddenly, a dapper fellow came in, late for the show. Dapper isn't even the word for him. James Bond circa 1963 might do. Overcoat and bowler hat; full suit, vest, tie, razor-cut hair. Hell, all he needed were spats. And as Swingin' London Bob bopped snappily into the room, the two warriors turned and froze in their tracks, staring with obvious astonishment. They were so amazed that they didn't even say anything funny.

The mod took his seat, and the warriors and I settled back down to enjoy Joe Ely, when the point of this story came along. Out of the shadows came the blind man, being bumped into and stopping in the half-dark, feeling around him with his cane, squinting up at the lights, which must have seemed a mile away to him. The handsome warrior, who turned out to be named Dave, turned and stared at the man. His face was expressionless as he watched what was obviously a struggle. The blind man started toward us again, trying to get through the chairs and bodies and tables and waitresses and wandering bikers. I watched Dave watch him. I watched him thinking about what he was watching. And I saw him decide to respond. He turned and put his beer on the low wall beside me, and he walked to the blind man and grabbed his arm. I heard him say, "Are you okay?"

"I'm trying to find somewhere to stand away from the noise!" the man shouted, smiling at the air ten inches above Dave's head.

And Dave put his arm around the man's waist. He put his arm around the man's waist tenderly. He put his arm tight around the man's waist like a lover and said, "It's all right. You're all right."

And he took the man in his arms and said, "Just back up with me." And he backed him out of the way and leaned him safely on the wall, then looked at me and said to the man, "Let's move this way just a little bit so these guys can see. You're all right. I've got you." And he eased the man into place.

Dave the Warrior, scourge of the roadhouse, scaring all

the bad boys, showed mercy. He didn't have pity, because then he would have just watched and said *Aw how sad*. No, pity is just self-indulgence; it's show business. Mercy, however, is an active thing, it is a verb.

He reached across the gulf between them and took the man in his arms. All race, all regret, all rage, all gender, all macho, gone. Just for a moment. And God stepped into the room. Make no mistake, the Holy Ghost was there as Joe Ely rocked and Dave's partner sipped beer. Dave the Warrior did exactly what I have been trying and hoping to achieve in everything I write. He reminded me that it is all, everything we hope, possible.

Spring

Live in simple faith . . .
just as this trusting cherry
flowers, fades, and falls.
—*Issa*

Mr. Francis Brown, the great Arapaho medicine man, played a joke on me. At the same time, he taught me one of those Zen lessons wise men regularly dole out to us. Thich Nhat Hanh says: "If we take steps without anxiety, in peace and joy, then we . . . will cause a flower to bloom on the earth with every step." That's Mr. Brown: he's got a garden in his cowboy boots.

We were at a party out near Lyons. Mr. Brown had stepped outside to light up a smoke. Like an acolyte, I followed him out. I'd been following him around at about forty paces all weekend. He glanced at me out of the corner of his eye. Nodded. I nodded back.

"Hey," he said.

"Mr. Brown," I replied.

I didn't have a cigarette to light, so I busied myself kicking stones and looking around.

He tipped back his cowboy hat and squinted at me.

"Hey," he said again.

I looked up.

He gestured at the moon with his cigarette.

"See that moon?"

It was pale and full.

I nodded.

"Indian people come from up there," he said.

Wow! I thought. *The medicine man is teaching me a secret! A creation story! An Arapaho legend!*

"Really?" I finally said.

"Yeah," he nodded. Then he started pointing at the vivid craters scattered all across the moon's face. "Don't you see them teepee rings we left all over the place?"

He smiled slyly. Then he started to laugh at me.

We both stood there, cracking up. Those old Indian guys, they love to pull a leg. Still, when you think about it, that one small moment laughing together will probably live more vividly in my memory than some revelation.

And the message was also in the laughter.

I was looking for some fabulous *meaning,* some cosmic secret so I could peek *inside* of things. I wanted knowledge I had not earned. And in spite of this obvious New Age illumination-shopping, Mr. Brown gave me a good long look at what was more important: what was *there.* All the while, a fine and round and glowing lovely moon hung above me like a jewel. Mr. Brown reminded me to look, to be still, and to remember that the moon could be funny, too.

The other day the strangest and saddest thing happened. I couldn't believe I was there to see it. I was stunned by the whole scene.

I was doing my Mr. Quick five-mile hike up Boulder Creek Canyon and back. I go steaming up the mountains then drift back down enjoying the cliffs and the tiny rapids and the sun. Anyway, the top mile or two is dirt. The rest, from the bottom to this point, is paved. Health-crazed in-line skaters skate uphill till they hit the dirt.

So I was coming down the hill, and there's a tunnel right where you get to the pavement. Near the tunnel is a bench. You can sit on the bench and watch rock climbers stuck to the cliffs across the creek.

Sitting on this bench was a man who looked like he was

probably my age. You know—incredibly young, vibrant, virile. That age. And his little boy was on his lap. I'd say he was about five or six. They both wore in-line skates, and being an orphan now, of course I was attuned to the sweetness of the scene. They were watching the climbers, and Dad was explaining to Son what they were doing.

I went by, through the tunnel, started down. A group of junior high teens on a class nature hike was staggering down, too. All the kids winded from actually getting out of their seats and walking two miles. Bike riders were going both ways. Then, along came Dad and Son on their skates. Dad, behind me, was gently admonishing Son: "Watch out. Okay. Put on your brakes. Put on your brakes." They passed me. Everybody happy. The boy carried a hockey stick.

Here's where the universe played one of its ugly little jokes.

Dad got off balance after he passed me, and he skated into the dirt at the side of the trail, waving his arms to stay upright. He said, "I'm telling you to watch it and look at me" or something to that effect. Son, suddenly overcome with daring, perhaps because he was out-skating Dad, took off down the path, holding his hockey stick like he was on the ice, crying, "Oh boy, Dad!"

I glanced back at Dad.

In that instant, the unlikeliest tragedy took place: Son lost his balance and started to windmill his arms. At the same instant, a group of mountain-bikers was coming around the bend. Son sped into the second rider, a woman. To stop himself, he put out his hands. His fingers went into the spokes of her rolling front tire before she could stop herself. She crushed all his fingers under the front fork of the bike, where they jammed tight in the metal.

What impossible mathematical equation brought the vectors of Dad & Son & Bike Rider together? What improbable geometry took all the possible space in the Rocky Mountains, factored, squared, divided and square-rooted it to bring *that* boy's fingers into the space occupied by *that* bicycle at *that* speed on *that* afternoon?

Screaming.

They all collected, prying the wheel back off the crushed fingers. Joggers tearing down the hill to their cars, a mile away, to come for the boy and take him to a hospital. The shaken woman still on her bike seat, pouring water onto the tangle of fingers, easily as terrified as the swooning boy. Dad in charge and putting off his own shaking fit until they could get to an emergency room. The terrible fact of his phone call to Mom still before him.

I could not believe that I was probably the only one in the picture who had watched the entire story. I wondered later if Dad and Son would even remember the serenity of their moment sitting in the slanting sun. I wondered if I, who didn't matter at all, was the only witness who would remember the tenderness before the chaos.

I got a fan letter from a stranger. She had written:

> *5'7", pair of 38D's that have never seen*
> *the inside of a brassiere . . . I love expensive*

*perfumes, body oils . . . a man who has a lot of
confidence in his own sensuality . . . Take me with
you when you're feeling down. Let the sense
just surround you and wrap you up, protected.*

Her name was M.

I drove around the plains on a cold day, trying out this M-wrapper. She felt good. I ended up at the optimistically named "Walden Ponds," some sort of flooded quarry or strip mine. I ate a sandwich and watched evil weather come down off the Divide. Squadrons of migratory birds swirled and landed. I sipped coffee. I thought about those 38D's. I got out of the Jeep.

A tall gent in a baseball cap and binoculars around his neck stepped up to me and said, "You're probably not a birder, but there is a green-backed crane over there!"

I nodded appreciatively while grinning like an idiot to demonstrate my enthusiasm.

"Once in a rare while!" he exulted.

"Indeed!" I bellowed.

"Let me get my scope," the birder said, "so you can see him!"

"Okay!" I cried, whipped up into a false frenzy of green-backed crane mania.

The man rushed to his car, popped the trunk, and produced a green army scope on a tripod. He was smiling the whole time he assembled it, aimed it, focused it, and said, "There you are." He stepped back. I have never seen a happier man. He demonstrated the control knob on top of the scope: we gave it a trial turn together.

"Got it," I said, then bent to the task.

There it was! A green-backed crane stood slightly shimmering on the far shore. It stood perfectly still, fierce eyes watching the shallows for an unfortunate crawdad to show itself. Its back was quite vividly green. Its whole body formed the letter S.

My birding compadre had horn-rimmed glasses and short gray-peppered hair.

"There's a female ringneck," he said, smiling. The whole pond was a high school reunion ball for him. "Of course," he demurred, "there is no visible ring."

His voice was sonorous, singing a basso aria of waterfowl. We presided over a confabulation: geese, mallards, cranes, grebes, plovers, pelicans, gulls. "Of course," he reminded me, "there's no such thing as a *sea* gull." We chuckled knowingly.

I found myself sinking into his reverie. It grew silent out there under the clouds. We imagined their immense journeys. If given a choice at that moment, I believe we both would have sprouted wings and flown.

The sweet birder was moved to a strange silence. I backed away from him and went to the Jeep. My last sight of him: he stood on a point of land, binocs pressed to his eyes, scanning the troops, like a general who had fallen in love with his army.

I pulled M. close again and sped out onto the plains, doing seventy-five and listening to Blue Cheer as loud as the speakers could stand it.

Coffee always promises to be good, but it isn't. Sex always thrills in anticipation, promising to be good, but it often isn't.

Driving 1,000 miles in the middle of the week when everybody else is working is just the thing that should be very good, but it sometimes isn't. I think the only thing I can count on tonight at 2:30 A.M., the only thing always good, the only thing that will not let you down, is the crickets.

The other day, as I was walking along Boulder Creek, grinding uphill like a tractor, I came upon an ingratiating scene. A nerdy looking fellow was standing in front of me, right in the middle of the path, still as a fossil. He was bent at the waist, hands on knees. I thought at first he was sick, or winded and trying to catch his breath. His lower body was obstructed by the bushes at the turn in the trail.

The whole scene revealed itself as I came around the bend: he wasn't throwing up or gasping—he was looking at the ground. Sticking out of the bushes, stretched out straight and unmoving as a whittled branch, was a slim and young-looking rattlesnake. It looked like a mottled yardstick pointed directly at the man.

Both of them were frozen in place, staring at each other. Each one, in his own way, looked simply astounded. No threats, no panicking, no rattling. They just stood there, totally focused, regarding each other with great curiosity. I veered close to them and slowed as I passed so I could gawk at their little science experiment. Neither of them paid me any mind. Nobody stirred. I passed by and walked along feeling oddly cheerful, filled with good will.

A few days later, as I was driving to Denver on the highway, a big old car shot by me, then slammed on its brakes and skidded to the shoulder, where it kicked up a huge cloud of dust. The passenger door flew open, and a long-haired fellow in a paroxysm of rage flew out, screaming and threatening the driver. He slammed the door as hard as humanly possible. The woman driving floored it, swerving madly into traffic and burning rubber going one way, while he stomped off at a near trot into oncoming cars, heading the opposite direction. Hatred. Tears. The shakes. Another microcosmic American tragedy.

Now, it seems too obvious a point to even make. And it sticks in my craw to be this groovy. But if a man and a rattler can get along, why can't two humans get along? If a man can resist panic when he sees a serpent, somehow not pick up a rock and crush the snake's head—and the snake (all right, it was probably still groggy from the cold) can resist panic and not shake its rattles, or coil in a threat display, or even strike— why is it then that two humanoids cannot keep from poisoning each other, from taking Cain's stone and striking the other down?

Midnight. Late Spring.

I'm a pretty good teacher. I'm a sucker for trying to make someone else's dreams come true. Only I'm focusing on my own dreams this time. In the past I took care of everyone but me. It's time for me to learn to put my arm around my own shoulders and lead myself out of the pain.

I'm walking down National Avenue, heart of the ghetto. I'm looking for little Luis. He's here somewhere, on this street, all alone. He's been molested, and nobody cares. He's been beat up, and nobody knows. His house is full of hate and fear. The thugs have found and killed all his pets. He has nothing, and he fears he will never have anything again. And that mad black boy with the knife wants to stab him. And his own siblings never come to see him. And he's only seven, but he's sure no one is ever going to like him. And when he got molested, he blew up like a balloon, and his father hated him for it, found ways to beat the shit out of him to make him tough.

In his world, when he got lit matches stuck in his mouth, fusing his lips shut in one corner (a "joke" gone awry), he had to apologize to them for crying and making the family feel bad.

It's hard to believe he's me.

He's on one of these yellow lawns, between these low-rent collapsing apartment blocks. I know I can find him. He's playing with a wind-up squirrel, a little mechanical toy that hops when you turn the key. It will soon break and go in the trash.

I have always hated this little scared boy. I was always ashamed of him. But he didn't do anything. He got buried in an avalanche. He got hit by a tornado. How could he know what to do? How could he know where to find sanctuary?

So he made a billion-dollar gift and buried it for me because he couldn't save himself. But he had Teresita's blood in him: he could see *me*. Thirty-some years down the road, in a future he didn't think he would see, he could see me. So he buried the nugget of his soul, deep, where the pressure and the heat turned it into a gem, and that gem came out for me in words, writing, books, stories, novels, poems. He knew enough about me to know I wouldn't be able to resist digging for it.

I think he was hoping the gift he gave me would someday make me come and save him. He wanted to walk in the Rockies. He wanted to stand before a deer and watch it slowly step forward, its nostrils opening and closing as it sniffed the air and wondered who he was and what he was doing there. He always dreamed of snow. He always wanted to write a book. He wanted a new wind-up squirrel.

So I'm running down that God-forsaken street, that violent ugly street, and I'm looking for myself. And, I swear, if I can find me there, I'll pick myself up and run far away. And I'll try with all my might not to betray that boy again.

That's the plan.

We struggle in our mind and body, and we don't touch the peace and joy that are available right now—the blue sky, the green leaves, the eyes of our beloved . . . What is most important is to find peace and to share it with others. To have peace, you can begin by walking peacefully. Everything depends on your steps.

—*Thich Nhat Hanh*

. . . a boy
falls into his own soul
and out, like a plane
out of a tailspin.

—*Linda Hasselstrom*

I got nephew-sitting duty today.

Tommy, who posed with me for the back cover photo of *The Fever of Being,* went with me to get some lunch. He wanted Kentucky Fried. Off to the Chickery! While there, we were served by a very nice woman named Laverne. She had undergone throat surgery, and she could only talk by using one of those machines you hold to your throat that makes an electric voice-box vibration. Tommy had never seen or heard such a thing.

I think it really confounded him, but to his credit, he barely batted an eye—though I did notice him peering up at her in a sort of awe. When she spoke to him directly, he couldn't understand her. "What?" he'd say, and I'd translate.

It was a surreal scene, with Laverne talking to me about M. C. Hammer in her artificial voice, and me trying to remember that I didn't have to shout or speak slowly, that she could comprehend me perfectly well.

———————

Tommy wanted to go to a ghost town, so we drove over Flagstaff Mountain to Gross Reservoir, and down the dirt road around back, and up in 4WD, and parked this side of Coal Creek Canyon in a roadside dirt lot. I pointed out a sign warning hikers about mountain lions. We laughed about it, how the sign would have given his mom a heart attack. But we were he-men. We weren't afraid of lions!

Then he said, "Uncle Weess, are there really lions here?"

"Nah!" I bellowed. "That sign's there just in case!"

"Just in case. . . . "

"Right!"

As soon as we started to walk, we stumbled upon a deer's fetlock. It was the end of a foreleg, obviously ripped from its body by a lion. The protruding end of the leg-bone was white. The hoof and the tan hide clung to the rest of it like a glove. It was delicately angled, bent into an *L*.

I picked it up just to get a hold of the kill. Feel the certainty of it. Tommy thought that was simply too gross to deal with.

"You're *touching* it?" he cried.

"Sure," I said. I offered it to him. "Want to feel it?"

"No way! Wash your hands!"

I was surprised—I thought the leftovers of a gory lion kill were the essence of boyness.

I stuck it in my back pocket like a comb. Tommy was thirty-eight; I was seven.

————————————

The gray wood skeleton of a cabin. Bits of pine board still hammered to stout gray cross-beams looked, from a distance, like moss beards, tatters of cloth. We used Tommy's pocket knife to dig old bullets out of the timbers.

————————————

Later, Tommy continued to renew my faith in general boyism by being appalled enough by an ancient outhouse to give it a detailed investigation, peering into the dirt pit for signs of petrified poop. After his inspection, he carved his initials into the wood.

We decided to follow the old wagon ruts that meandered past the settlement and into the woods. They could be seen sketching their way through the meadow grasses in the distance, angling down toward the plains. Denver a small smoky coral reef far away.

The ruts were full of soft dust. We wandered on and off them, filling our socks with stickers, and we sat in the dirt like two Cub Scouts and picked them out.

Our meadow was wildflower bright.

Up in the trees, nearby train tracks making a silver hiss and rusty clack as a motorized something climbed the grade out of Denver. We walked about a half mile. We turned back. And where the twin wagon ruts widened to a sandy gap, near the ruins of a barn: fresh lion tracks.

Four clear tracks, big, sharp, puggy, perfectly clear tracks that could have been lifted right out of a field guide. They were about as wide as tarantulas. Cutting across our path at an angle. Following us.

I looked around, felt the trees alive with curiosity. We'd been brought into a Presence. Something utterly remarkable in the world had come along and cut across our path. Our world had been intercepted by Wildness. It was watching us. They're curious, our cousins, and I've heard of them following people for miles, watching us do our mysterious thing. What do they think? What do they want?

It might have been stalking us, who knows. I looked at Tommy, and I saw a perfect meal for a lion.

His hair was the brightest gold.

You are not eating my nephew, I thought.

I rested my hand on the back of his neck—damp with sweat, thin as a fawn's—and we walked back through the meadows together.

about the author

Wandering Time is Luis Alberto Urrea's seventh book. His others are *Across the Wire* and *By the Lake of Sleeping Children* (nonfiction); *In Search of Snow* (fiction); *The Fever of Being* and *Ghost Sickness* (poetry); and *Nobody's Son* (memoir). Urrea has been awarded the Western States Book Award, the Colorado Book Award, and the Christopher Award. He also has been anthologized widely, and his work can be found in *The Best American Poetry, 1996; Resist Much, Obey Little: Some Thoughts on Ed Abbey; Muy Macho;* and *The Late Great Mexican Border.*

Urrea is Writer in Residence at the University of Southwestern Louisiana in Lafayette. He is completing a historical novel on Teresita Urrea, the Saint of Cabora.